Published by
the International Debate Education
Association

For permission to reproduce in whole or
in part please contact:
idea@idebate.org

ISBN 0-9702130-0-X

Written by William Driscoll

Design by vBUREAU.com

Publication of this handbook and
other IDEA activities are made
possible by the generous support of
the Open Society Institute and
the Network of Soros Foundations.

Special thanks to Ken Broda-Bahm,
Vlad Galushko, Michael Gately,
Liz Lorant, Anca Pusca, Noel Selegzi,
Charles Temple, Nina Watkins,
Marcin Zaleski, the Reading & Writing
for Critical Thinking Project,

AND

all the members of IDEA
who have contributed to this project.

idea

**international
debate
education
association**

www.idebate.org

discovering
the world through
DEBATE

A practical
guide to
EDUCATIONAL DEBATE
for debaters,
coaches
and judges

Table of Contents.

Foreword.
The Karl Popper Debate Program and the International Debate Education Association

The subject of this handbook is educational debate. Specifically, it deals with a particular format of educational debate, one that is named after the noted philosopher Karl Popper, who was born in Austria and spent most of his life teaching and writing in England. In one of his most famous works, *The Open Society and its Enemies* (1945), Popper said that he believed in the existence of absolute truth, but was suspicious of anyone who claimed to possess it. Popper argued that knowledge progresses in increments and that conclusions are provisional. He believed that theses are developed so that they may be discussed; that critical thinking is a collaborative process of dialogue and public discussion; and that knowledge progresses by conjecture and refutation, by the rigorous public testing of ideas and opinions. Educational debate is an activity that puts Popper's ideas into practice. Students who participate in educational debate learn to think critically about problems and issues in the world beyond the classroom. They learn skills that are necessary for active participation in a deliberative democracy.

The Open Society Institute and Soros Foundations Network established the Karl Popper Debate Program in 1994 to encourage critical thinking, personal expression, and tolerance for different opinions. Since then, it has helped introduce debate to more than 60,000 students and 15,000 teachers in high schools and universities in more than two dozen countries: Albania, Azerbaijan, Belarus, Bosnia and Herzegovina, Bulgaria, the Czech Republic, Estonia, Georgia, Haiti, Hungary, Kazakhstan, Kyrgyzstan, Latvia, Lithuania, Macedonia, Moldova, Mongolia, Poland, Romania, Russia, Slovakia, Slovenia, Tajikistan, Ukraine, Uzbekistan, and Yugoslavia. Participating students debate, for the most part, in their native languages, including minority languages in countries with significant minority populations. They use English, Russian, or other languages for international competition.

The **centerpiece of the Program is an international summer camp**, where students and teachers from each of the participating countries gather for two weeks of seminars and debating on an important contemporary topic. In each participating country, the program proceeds on an annual development cycle. A group of teachers is trained in debate, which is presented as a method of teaching critical thinking skills. These training teams are responsible for establishing the program in their own schools, and for training teachers from other schools. Students who graduate from schools where debate programs have been established are encouraged to continue their involvement by acting as judges or as coaches, or by forming debate clubs at their universities. In each participating country, the program also helps to establish a nongovernmental organization that helps organize, promote, and sustain debate activities, and also coordinates instruction and competition.

The **International Debate Education Association (IDEA)** was created in 1999 to coordinate and promote interaction among the debate programs in the various countries of operation, and with other international debate organizations. In order to promote the growth of debate, IDEA has undertaken a variety of initiatives. It has produced **training videos** and materials. It has established centers in participating countries **to provide debaters with access to research materials, the Internet** (where possible), and photocopiers. It has created debate listserves and a web site to offer access to curricula and links to libraries and free media. It publishes a newsletter that offers additional training materials and acts as a forum for students and teachers to exchange ideas. And finally, it has produced **this handbook, which is intended to explain the nature of debate, and to offer a practical guide for participants and organizers.**

Introduction,
How to Use This Handbook

This handbook provides a comprehensive guide to Karl Popper Debate, a format of educational debate developed by the Open Society Institute and the Soros Foundations Network. We discuss the nature of political debate and present a series of practical rules and guidelines for debaters. Many audiences will find this text useful: debaters, coaches, judges, parents, school administrators, and spectators. We recognize that our various audiences will have different degrees of familiarity with debate. Some readers will be new practitioners; others will be experienced coaches. The corollary is that this book will have different uses for different readers, and it was written with that in mind.

This handbook begins with a discussion of the roots of educational debate, and tries to explain the role of debate in an open society. This discussion, we believe, is valuable for all readers, at every level of experience. Karl Popper Debate can best be understood in the light of this discussion. The book then shifts from the theoretical to the practical. We offer a brief description of the format followed in an educational debate, to provide some orientation for the pragmatic directives that follow. This overview, while essential for the neophyte, will be familiar to more experienced participants.

Our first two chapters, in a sense, describe a final destination. They **outline the shape of an educational debate**, in the Karl Popper format, and explain why it exists. With **the third chapter**, we begin a description of the journey to that destination. That is, we talk about the **preparation** that precedes the debate event. This description will be of most interest to those who are making the journey: debaters and their coaches. The journey starts with the resolution proposed for competition. **The resolution is analyzed in our third chapter**. We have tried to articulate the nature of a good resolution—so this chapter should be of interest even to experienced coaches, who are expected to help league administrators write resolutions for competitions. We follow the definition of the resolution with an account of practical approaches used by coaches and debaters to generate logical arguments either for or against the resolution. Debaters should find this discussion illuminating, but it will be of greatest value to coaches and teachers who are looking for ways to help students to prepare.

The preparation for **a debate event culminates in** the creation and refinement of **a case**, or a series of cogent arguments relating to the resolution. This book offers a discussion of what factors make a case strong or weak. This discussion is followed by a more general account of logical strategies and logical errors. These discussions are, we think, of vital interest for debaters and coaches. Judges, who must develop an understanding of the validity of logical strategies, should also review them.

The center of this book is a step-by-step examination of a debate. We describe the nature and purpose of each section of a debate in the Karl Popper format. More importantly, we discuss the tactical choices that must be made by debaters during the course of the debate itself. This discussion is grounded on the transcript of an actual debate, a championship match held in 1997. Debaters should find this material most helpful, but coaches and judges, too, should benefit from this analysis. All readers may find it valuable to review the transcript, if not the commentary, before and while reading the body of the text.

The final chapters of the book are directed at specific audiences. Chapter 12, on rhetoric and style, consists mostly of practical advice for debaters; this advice, of course, will also be valuable for coaches and judges. Chapter 13, about the debate club in the school community, is meant primarily for coaches and teachers who are setting up a team, but it should also be helpful to parents and school administrators. The final chapter, about the role of the judge, has an obvious audience. Debaters don't need to read this chapter—but many of them, who are curious about why they win and why they lose, will probably want to.

I may be wrong
and you may be right,
but with an effort
we may get nearer
to the truth.

—Karl Popper

Chapter 1.
The Roots of Educational Debate

This handbook is designed to be practical. Among other things, it will tell you how to establish a debate team, how to prepare for a debate and how to judge a competition. But before we discuss such practical matters, it is important to talk about the nature of educational debate. What is educational debate, and what is the value of the activity? To answer those questions, we can begin by considering the nature of debate in the world beyond the classroom. Then we can look at the ways that educational debate is similar to other forms of debate, and the ways that it is different.

DEBATE AND DEMOCRACY

Debate is an essential activity in democratic societies. More than two thousand years ago, when democracy first flourished in Athens, citizens met regularly in public assemblies. Their votes determined the policy and the actions of their state. They decided whether Athens should go to war, and how it should fight. They created laws, which directed the course of daily life for citizens. But their votes were always preceded by debate. Citizens and leaders argued about what was right for Athens. They argued about was morally right and about what was legal. They argued about the best way to achieve a desired outcome. They argued about what was possible, and what was prudent.

Today, debate is still essential to democracy. The democratic process has changed and continues to evolve, but debates continue. Some debates are conducted in legislative assemblies; some are held in lecture halls and public arenas; some are presented in schools and universities; others can be read in the columns of magazines and newspapers, or heard on radio or television. Like their predecessors from earlier centuries, citizens argue about what is best for their societies, and shape the course of law, policy, and action.

We can understand this model better, perhaps, by considering other models. In some societies, the course of the state is shaped by power. Those who have absolute power—and it doesn't matter whether that means kings or emperors or aristocrats or military juntas or totalitarian governments—direct the course of the state as they see fit. They hold exclusive power. Popular debate has no meaningful role in such societies.

In democracies, however, power belongs to the people. In John Locke's famous formulation, governments derive their legitimate power from the consent of the governed. Citizens direct the course of the state, but they do not always agree. They may have conflicting interests. They may have different ways of understanding a common problem. They may have different priorities, and different ideas about what is most important. They may have different understandings of what is right. In short, there are such things as **debatable propositions**—that is, propositions about which reasonable people can disagree.

DEBATE IS A FORM OF PERSUASION THAT CAN PRODUCE CONSENSUS

It is in this context that debate is essential and vital. Debate is not simply a form of expression. Rather, it is a form of persuasion. The debater hopes to change minds. She hopes that listeners will come to see things her way. Debate does not produce immediate unanimity. Over time, it can produce consensus, and a changed understanding of what is right and best. One issue that illustrates this is slavery. In classical Greece, slavery was not a debatable proposition. Aristotle, for example, thought it was a natural result of racial or social superiority. But some two thousand years later, in the United States, it was a hotly debated issue. On one side were those who saw slavery as a violation of the slave's natural right to liberty. On the other side were those who argued for the primacy of a citizen's right to own property, and his right to manage his private property without government interference. Today, of course, the issue is not debatable, because slavery is regarded as a categorically unacceptable violation of the right to personal liberty. But that recognition—that common consensus—is the product of centuries of debate. Other examples abound. The modern concepts of free speech, self-determination, and justifiable war are all the products of debate.

Citizens disagree in democracies, but not all disagreements are the same. Some disagreements are limited and practical; others are broad and abstract. What is a limited, practical disagreement? Let's say, for example, that a country's legislature is trying to decide whether to permit the importation of genetically altered food. There are immediate practical concerns about the safety of such food. The legislature must decide whether it poses a risk to its inhabitants. But it also must decide whether the risk is acceptable or unacceptable. Even if it concludes that there is a risk, it must consider which citizens are affected. Does the genetically altered food present a risk to anyone who doesn't eat it? Would it be acceptable, then, to import the food with a warning label, and let consumers make their own choices? If the genetically altered food is allowed, does that mean that genetically altered crops can be grown in the country? And what would be the potential impact of such crops on the country's ecosystem? At the same time, the legislators must think about the economic impact of importing such food. If the food is banned, are alternative foods less expensive or more expensive? Would banning such imports impose a financial burden on the citizens? And what would be the other consequences of such a ban? What would happen if the exporting country started to impose its own bans in retaliation?

This example could be developed further, but this sketch should make it easy to see the kinds of conflicts that would arise. In the end, a practical decision must be made about importing food. But that decision must consider cost, impact on the community, and impact on the environment, among other things. Debate will help to clarify those issues before a decision is made.

The example above, as noted, is a limited, practical debate. At the other end of the spectrum, we could place the debate about slavery. Of course, there were practical issues involved in that debate. What are the economic implications of freeing the slaves? If slaves continue to do the same work, who will pay them and how much? And so on. But the practical questions in this debate were comparatively unimportant: the slavery debate was, ultimately, abstract. That is, it was a debate about what is morally right, rather than about what is practical or cost-effective.

DEBATE IS AIMED AT CLARIFYING THE NATURE OF CONFLICTS

Most debates in the society at large fall somewhere between those two extremes. They are not purely practical; neither are they purely theoretical. Indeed, the process of debate is aimed at clarifying the nature of conflicts. On the one hand, debate demonstrates the practical ramifications of theoretical positions. On the other hand, and more important, it illuminates the conflicts between abstract principles that often lie behind practical issues.

Let us look at another example, a controversial event from recent history. In 1999 and the first half of the year 2000, there was considerable debate over the treatment of General Auguste Pinochet, the former leader of Chile. The facts, briefly, are as follows. General Pinochet came to power in 1973, as the leader of a military coup that overthrew the government of President Salvador Allende. Shortly after taking power, Pinochet imprisoned thousands of his opponents. During his time as leader, thousands more were imprisoned, and many were never seen again. Pinochet remained in control of the government until 1989, when democratic elections were restored. When he lost the election to Patricio Aylwin, he relinquished power and retired from the presidency. He retained control of the military, however, and was given the title of Senator for Life. In 1999, Pinochet traveled to England, where he sought medical treatment that was unavailable in Chile. While in England, Pinochet was indicted by a Spanish court on charges of human rights violations. The Spanish courts argued that they had the right to indict Pinochet because of international treaties concerning human rights which both Spain and England had signed. The government of Spain called for his extradition, so that he could be tried for those crimes, committed while he was in office.

The British government—along with the rest of the world—debated the merits of the Spanish request. In making its request, the Spanish government invoked the concept of inalienable human rights, as guaranteed by treaties to which both Spain and Britain are signatories. By definition, human rights are distinct from legal rights and other rights. They are rights possessed by all human beings, no matter where they live, and no matter under what form of government. The following examples may clarify this distinction. The right to trial by jury, for instance, is a legal right, guaranteed by certain governments under certain circumstances; however, the right to liberty—that is, the right not to be enslaved, or imprisoned without cause—is the birthright of all human beings. Human rights have been articulated and invoked countless times in the modern era. Human rights were articulated in a United Nations declaration of 1948, and formed the moral core of the Helsinki accords signed by the world's leading powers in 1975.

According to the Spanish government, compelling evidence suggested that General Pinochet had violated the rights of Chilean citizens. A trial to determine his guilt or innocence was imperative, as a matter of justice. But that was only one side of the debate. On the other side was another powerful and widely accepted axiom of contemporary geopolitics, the principle of national sovereignty. According to this principle, every country is free to rule itself, without the interference or intervention of other countries. Most obviously, an act of military aggression is a violation of a country's sovereignty—but it does not take an act of physical force to constitute a violation. In the case of Pinochet, it was argued that allowing the general to stand trial in Spain would have constituted a violation of Chile's national sovereignty. General Pinochet, after all, was not an escaped criminal sought by the legal system of his own country. He was, rather, a man with diplomatic credentials, recognized as the legitimate leader of Chile by the world community during his reign. He turned power over to his successors in an orderly fashion. To put it simply, the government of Chile did not seek the trial or punishment for General Pinochet. Moreover, they argued, only the government of Chile, and the people of Chile, had the right to hold General Pinochet accountable for his actions.

In the end, the general was allowed to return to Chile, escaping extradition to and trial in Spain. The British government asserted that he was mentally unfit to stand trial, and allowed him to return to Chile. Many observers viewed this as a compromise, rather than as an act of compassion or justice. The case is, nevertheless, instructive. The question of whether Pinochet should have been extradited remains a debatable proposition. There are valid principles involved on both sides. Reasonable people can and do disagree about it.

KARL POPPER DEBATE WAS CREATED WITH THE IDEALS OF DEBATE IN SOCIETY AT LARGE IN MIND

On one level, the treatment of General Pinochet was a practical and diplomatic problem for the countries involved. But it was a case that legitimately involved every country in the world, because it exemplified a conflict of universal, axiomatic principles. Should the principle of national sovereignty be deemed inviolable? Perhaps—but there are corollaries that follow from such a decision. If sovereignty is inviolable, then the world has no right ever to interfere within the sovereign boundaries of any country, no matter how a government is treating its people. But what is the result if human rights are judged to be of greater importance than sovereignty, in all cases? Might not such a judgment allow powerful nations to impose their wills on the governments of weaker countries?

FROM DEBATE IN SOCIETY AT LARGE TO EDUCATIONAL DEBATE

The foregoing discussion has attempted to describe the role of debate in the world beyond the classroom—specifically, in democratic societies—and to examine the nature of the conflicts debated there. The next order of business is to explain the connection between debate in a democratic society and the competitive debates in the Karl Popper format.

First, it must be said that Karl Popper Debate was created with the ideals of debate in the society at large in mind. It recognizes that debate is a vital part of a democratic tradition. It is an activity that aims to find answers to important social questions. The program does not see debate as a mere game, or as a simple contest of rhetorical skill. Rather, it views debate as a valid and demanding intellectual exercise. Participants in debate are asked to think critically about questions that are important and real. Debaters learn to understand the principles that underlie conflicting policies. They learn how to weigh the merits of conflicting principles; they learn the difference between argumentation and mere sophistry.

THE DIFFERENCES BETWEEN DEBATE IN SOCIETY AT LARGE AND EDUCATIONAL DEBATE

The differences between debate in society at large debate and educational debate are differences of form. Educational debate is characterized by formality of structure, restriction of conflict, and competitive judgment. Finally, it is distinctive in that debaters must argue both sides of a given proposition.

It will be seen that some of these differences are comparatively insignificant. Take, for example, the formal structure of educational debate. Sometimes, of course, other forms of debates lack formal structure. The newspaper editor writing a column does not have to obey any formal rules. But very often, these debates are highly structured. In televised debates, candidates for public office sometimes must obey time limits when answering questions posed by journalists. Legislative debates are usually governed by parliamentary rules of order. Karl Popper Debate is formal, rather than formless. The debate is divided into ten distinct sections, each with its own rules, and each limited to a specific length of time.

EDUCATIONAL DEBATE IS CHARACTERIZED BY FORMALITY OF STRUCTURE, RESTRICTION OF CONFLICT, AND COMPETITIVE JUDGEMENT

A lack of formal structure is often mirrored by a loose definition of conflict. It's true that some debates are sometimes tightly focused (as when the legislature must debate about whether to import genetically altered foods), but very often the debatable proposition is not clearly stated. In educational debate, the proposition must be clearly and explicitly stated. The technical term used is *resolution*. A resolution is a proposition with which debaters agree or disagree. The resolution might be this: "Resolved: Capital punishment should be abolished." One team is designated as affirmative, and argues in favor of this statement. The other team is designated as negative, and argues against it. These terms will be discussed in detail in the following chapters.

As in the larger world, debate resolutions will vary in the degree of abstraction they contain. Sometimes, the debate resolution will be very specific: for example, "Resolved that Hungary should join NATO." Sometimes, however, the resolutions will be more abstract: for example, "Resolved that genetic engineering is unethical." Whatever the formulation of the resolution, however, a debate in the Popper format is aimed at clarifying conflicts of principles, rather than merely practical concerns.

EDUCATIONAL DEBATE DIFFERS FROM OTHER FORMS OF DEBATE IN THAT DEBATERS MUST ARGUE BOTH SIDES OF THE SAME PROPOSITION

Another difference is that Karl Popper Debate is competitive. But that is not, at bottom, a huge difference. In other areas of society debates are often followed by votes: for candidates, or policies, or laws. All debaters are interested in persuading their listeners. Educational debaters are interested in persuading their judges. The judge's job is to decide which side—affirmative or negative—has been more persuasive during the debate. Finally, educational debate differs from other forms of debate in society in that debaters must argue both sides of the same proposition. This is a significant difference that warrants an extended discussion.

ARGUING BOTH SIDES

A debate competition consists of a number of rounds—in the first round, a team argues in favor of the resolution. In the second round, they meet a new opponent, and argue against the resolution. In the other walks of life, of course, such a reversal would be denounced as hypocrisy, and rightly so. Why, then, is such a reversal not only allowed, but also required, in educational debate? This question calls for a clearly articulated answer. We mean to show, in the following discussion, that arguing both sides of a resolution is far from a flaw in educational debate, but is instead one of the things that gives debate its intellectual value.

To reiterate a position that was discussed earlier: Debate is not about the conflict of good and evil; neither is it about the conflict between truth and falsehood, or between facts and opinions. Debate is, rather, about the conflict of values and principles. Taken independently, each value has worth and validity, and deserves support. But when two valid principles conflict, a decision must be made as to which is more important. Reasonable people will disagree about which is more important. There is something to be said for each side. That is the nature of a debatable proposition.

To put it another way, a good debate resolution has to have this kind of ambiguity. If the resolution is lopsided, there is no point in arguing it. The virtue of debating both sides of a good resolution is that debaters come to understand that there are different ways of thinking about the same issue. By understanding and appreciating both sides, debaters come to a better understanding of their own ideas. When faced with conflicts beyond the classroom, they make decisions that are informed and principled, rather than prejudiced and capricious.

ARGUING BOTH SIDES FORCES STUDENTS TO RECOGNIZE THAT THERE IS NO MONOPOLY ON TRUTH

In short, then, arguing both sides has considerable educational value. It forces students to recognize that, in everyday life, there is no monopoly on truth. A given individual may hold a belief with a passion that is founded on careful and serious thinking; that does not mean, however, that people who believe the opposite are not also careful and serious thinkers. To return to our earlier example, people who believe that General Pinochet should have stood trial in Spain cannot assume, in fairness, that anyone who believes otherwise is stupid, thoughtless, or unprincipled. They must, rather, accept the possibility that their opponents have thought about the issue as carefully as they have themselves.

As a corollary, students learn that if they want to change someone else's mind, the best way is to examine the opposing belief from the inside, and refute its premises. When students argue both sides of a resolution, they learn that both sides are worthy of serious considera- tion—even if, in their own hearts, they favor one over the other. If we are to arrive at the truth, said Karl Popper, it will be only after the careful consideration of many possibilities.

A MODEL: FROM SOCIAL CONFLICT TO EDUCATIONAL DEBATE

We will close this chapter by returning to an earlier example, one that should clarify the relationship between debate outside the confines of the classroom and educational debate. Let us return to the case of General Pinochet. It is possible to construct a debate resolution with specific reference to this conflict. That is, it would be quite possible to argue this resolution: "Resolved: Britain should extradite General Pinochet to stand trial in Spain." Very often in competition, however, current events will be used as a spring- board to more abstract propositions. As noted in our earlier discussion, one can see, in this crisis, a conflict between human rights and national sovereignty. So General Pinochet might inspire a resolution like this: "Resolved: The protection of human rights justifies direct foreign intervention into the domestic affairs of a sovereign nation." This resolution is inspired by one particular international crisis, but it is not confined to it. In arguing this resolution, students might consider General Pinochet, but they also might consider other crises, at other points in time. If the resolution is true, it is always true; and if it is false, it is always false—whether we are talking about Kosovo, Vietnam, Rwanda, or Latvia. When the resolution is framed abstractly, debaters are forced to think about the meaning of terms and principles, and how they apply in other situations. Say, for example, that we define self-determination as a human right. Does that mean, if we affirm the resolution, that it would be justified to take military action against a country that denied women the right to vote?

There are, of course, other principles and issues at play in the Pinochet crisis. In addi- tion to human rights and sovereignty. And different debate resolutions could be fashioned from the conflicts involved. For example: "Resolved: Leaders of nations can be held personally liable for the violation of citizens' rights." One thing would remain constant, however. The debate resolution would focus on the conflicts of principles and values that underlie most conflicts.

The point is this: When resolutions for educational debate are formulated in an abstract way, it does not mean that educational debate is artificial and distant from the rest of society. Rather, abstract resolutions force debaters to focus on the issues of value and principle that lie behind the conflicts which pervade contemporary society. As we see in our model debate, however, many resolutions remain firmly grounded in the larger society, and cannot be argued without a proper attention to facts as well as principles. Our model debate focuses on the legalization of marijuana. It must be argued as a conflict of principle, but the argument depends upon a careful understanding of the physical effects of using marijuana. See the appendix for the transcript and commentary of this debate.

In the chapters that follow, we will focus our attention on the rules and practices of educational debate. But we should never lose sight of what debate really is. It is an exercise that has its origins in the very roots of democracy, and draws its meaning from the debates over issue of concern to the world beyond the classroom.

Chapter 2.
A Structural Overview

In the chapters that follow, we will discuss the steps that must be taken to prepare for a debate. We will then offer a detailed account of each section of a round in Karl Popper Debate. At this point, we will describe the format in general terms, in order to create a context for what follows.

THE SECTIONS OF THE DEBATE ROUND

Obviously, there are two opposing sides that meet in a debate round. One side affirms the resolution, and one negates it. As we mentioned earlier, they exchange their opinions according to a strict format, which allows both sides an equal amount of time to present their positions. There are ten sections in the format. Each section has a defined purpose and a set of rules. Six of the sections consist of speeches—that is, uninterrupted presentations by a designated speaker. The remaining four sections consist of cross-examination—that is, a series of questions and answers involving one speaker from each side. The length of time allotted to each section is also determined by the format.

	Section	Time
1.	Affirmative Constructive (speech)	6 minutes
2.	First Negative Cross-Examination	3 minutes
3.	Negative Constructive (speech)	6 minutes
4.	First Affirmative Cross-Examination	3 minutes
5.	First Affirmative Rebuttal (speech)	5 minutes
6.	Second Negative Cross-Examination	3 minutes
7.	First Negative Rebuttal (speech)	5 minutes
8.	Second Affirmative Cross-Examination	3 minutes
9.	Second Affirmative Rebuttal (speech)	5 minutes
10.	Second Negative Rebuttal (speech)	5 minutes

We will explain the purposes and rules of each section when we consider them in detail. For now, suffice it to say that the basic arguments about the resolution are contained in the constructive speeches. In these speeches, debaters argue all of their reasons for affirming or negating the resolution. The remaining speeches, the rebuttals, are devoted to attack and defense tactics. In these speeches, debaters present objections to the arguments made by their opponents, and they defend their own arguments against their opponents' objections. In other words, the rebuttal speeches are not meant to introduce completely new arguments in support of the team's position. The cross-examination sections are used to clarify arguments, and to lay the groundwork for objections that will be made in the rebuttal speeches.

In some debate formats, competitive debate is a solo event: there is one person affirming the resolution, who faces one person negating it. The Popper format is distinctive in that it conceives of debate as a team activity. We should be clear that **team** does not mean everyone in a school who participates in the debate activity: that is, properly, the debate club. The team, rather, is the group of individuals who are competing together as a unit in a given competition. In the Karl Popper Debate format, this debate team is composed of three individuals. They stay together in every round throughout the course of the competition. As discussed earlier, they will be switching sides as the competition goes on. The competition consists of a series of debates or rounds. In some rounds, they will be arguing in favor of the resolution, while in some rounds they will be arguing against it.

THE POPPER FORMAT CONCEIVES OF DEBATE AS A TEAM ACTIVITY

THE DEBATE TEAM IS COMPOSED OF THREE INDIVIDUALS

In each round, of course, there are two teams that meet to compete. All in all, six debaters speak in a round: three form the affirmative team, and three form the negative team. The roles assumed by the various team members are determined by the format. The debater who presents the constructive speech for the affirmative team, for example, remains to answer the questions posed by the negative team in their first cross-examination. Then that debater steps down, while other members of the team take the lead for the rebuttal and cross-examinations that follow, and then comes back to the fore again to ask questions in the second affirmative cross-examination. We will now revisit the section chart, with the appropriate responsibilities added. In this chart, each debater is designated by a number—e.g., as Affirmative 1, Affirmative 2, etc. Traditionally, the designation of " 1" is given to the debater who presents the team's constructive argument—that explains why the first member of the negative team to take the floor is designated as " Negative 3." Although the first to speak in sequence, he is asking questions of the affirmative side, not presenting the negative case on its own. For ease of reference, these positions are often abbreviated as A1, A2, A3, N1, and so on.

Section	Time	Speaker
Affirmative Constructive	6 minutes	Affirmative 1
First Negative Cross-Examination	3 minutes	Affirmative 1 *answers* Negative 3 *asks*
Negative Constructive	6 minutes	Negative 1
First Affirmative Cross-Examination	3 minutes	Affirmative 3 *asks* Negative 1 *answers*
First Affirmative Rebuttal	5 minutes	Affirmative 2
Second Negative Cross-Examination	3 minutes	Affirmative 2 *answers* Negative 1 *asks*
First Negative Rebuttal	5 minutes	Negative 2
Second Affirmative Cross-Examination	3 minutes	Affirmative 1 *asks* Negative 2 *answers*
Second Affirmative Rebuttal	5 minutes	Affirmative 3
Second Negative Rebuttal	5 minutes	Negative 3

All in all, these sections amount to 44 minutes, and they are evenly distributed: each team controls 22 minutes of the debate. Those 22 minutes break down into 16 minutes of speaking (constructives and rebuttals) and six minutes of questioning (cross-examinations). The debaters' roles vary: Affirmative 1 appears in three sections, for a total of 12 minutes (six minutes speaking, three minutes answering questions, and three minutes asking them); Affirmative 2 and Affirmative 3 both appear in two sections, for a total of eight minutes (five minutes speaking, three minutes of questions). The responsibilities on the negative team are similarly divided.

In addition to the sections outlined above, each round includes 16 minutes of preparation time—eight minutes for each team. This time is not scheduled into any particular place in the sequence of sections; it is taken at the discretion of each team, in whatever amounts they desire. The negative team, for example, might use two minutes before the first negative cross-examination, another two before their constructive, another two before their first rebuttal, and so on.

Even though the responsibilities of the individual debaters vary, it would be a mistake to think of these roles as being specialized or discretely different. We cannot emphasize strongly enough that debate in the Karl Popper format is for teams. Individual debaters do not win events, teams do. The debate team can be compared to a relay team in a track event; yes, the members will perform individually, but they will be judged as a whole. The three members of the debate team are responsible for different aspects of one coherent argument, either for or against the resolution. They do not present three different, incompatible arguments.

> **TEAMWORK IS IMPORTANT BECAUSE INDIVIDUAL DEBATERS DO NOT WIN EVENTS, TEAMS DO**

At the risk of straining the metaphor, we would also say that, like relay runners, debaters must learn to pass the baton. As we will discuss in the next few chapters, successful argument depends on following through. An admission made during cross-examination by an opponent must be exploited in the speech that follows in the next section. But, as the structural table shows, the debater who has just conducted the questioning never gives the speech that follows. Take, for example, this early sequence: Negative 3 asks questions in the second section, but they must be pursued by Negative 1 in the constructive (the third section). Negative 3, for his part, will return in the final section of the debate to give the Second Negative Rebuttal. But his job then is not to talk about the questions he asked half an hour earlier; his job, rather, is to sum up all the arguments that have been made since that time.

There is another aspect of debate that becomes evident after a quick analysis of the structure. Debaters do not spend most of their time talking. They spend most of their time listening. And listening, we will add immediately, does not mean waiting to talk. The success of the team effort really depends on how well they listen. We will discuss, in a later chapter, the importance of **flowing** the debate—that is, taking notes on what is said. When debaters make written notes, their listening becomes active, not passive; they do a better job of grasping what is said. Moreover, the debater who is flowing the debate can start to sketch responses as his opponent is speaking. Flowing helps to form reactions.

In this context, it is clear that preparation time is also a vital time during the debate. As soon as a section ends, the team members must huddle and, literally, compare notes. In a minute or two, one member of the team will have to stand and begin the next section of the debate. During preparation time, his teammates must pass on their ideas and suggest a strategy for the next section. If the team members cannot work together efficiently during prep time, the whole debate will fall apart. Arguments will be not be made, and refutations will go unanswered. As we will describe in the next chapters, the ground for collaborative work must be laid during the working sessions and practices that precede the competition itself.

Chapter 3.
Understanding the Resolution

In the last chapter, we described the structure of competitive debate in general terms. Everything begins with the resolution, the debatable proposition that will be argued during the debate. In this chapter, we will begin by talking a bit about the nature of resolutions, and then we will talk at length about how debaters begin their preparation for competition.

THE RESOLUTION We have already discussed some of the defining characteristics of the resolution. To reiterate, it is a debatable proposition. It is a statement of value or policy about which reasonable people can disagree. It is not a statement of opinion (e.g. "Resolved: The greatest movie ever made is *Saturday Night Fever*.") Neither is it a statement of fact, in the narrowest sense. One cannot, strictly speaking, conduct a debate about what is the highest peak in the Himalayas. Along the same lines, it is not like a legal argument about truth. Granted, there is a kind of debate when the prosecutor says, "The defendant is guilty of murder," and the defense attorney says, "My client is innocent." But that is not a debatable proposition, where something valid can be said for each side. The defendant is either guilty or innocent— only one of the alternatives is valid. For a resolution to be suitable for debate, it has to involve a conflict of values or policies, with the understanding that each side has merit.

> THE RESOLUTION IS A STATEMENT OF VALUE OR POLICY ABOUT WHICH REASONABLE PEOPLE CAN DISAGREE

In the first chapter, we discussed the nature of debates in the world beyond formal, educational; some, we noted, are very practical; some, on the other hand, are abstract and theoretical. Most debates fall between those two extremes. Karl Popper Debate is also aimed at that middle ground.

Let's examine a few sample resolutions. We can start with one about education: "Resolved: The state should provide education only in its official language." Clearly, there is an element of policy involved in this resolution. If it is affirmed, then the state must take certain practical actions, which will have costs and which will have an impact on various parts of the community. And it is possible to argue about this resolution by focusing on that practical level. The affirmative side might argue, for example, that putting a multilingual policy into place would effectively double the size of the state's educational budget, and in order to implement the program, the state would be forced to cut programs in other areas, such as health and welfare. Even here, a value judgment is made: namely, that health programs are more important than multilingual education.

But it is also clear that there are abstract ideas that lie behind this proposition. What is the state's obligation to its citizens? What are the rights of its citizens? Is it reasonable for the state to have different ways of treating different groups of citizens? Are students who speak a non-official language being punished? Or is it fair for a country to make cultural unity a part of its national identity?

These are just some questions that might be asked. The recurring theme, you will note, is values. What is right? What is fair? What is good? That is what we mean by a higher level of abstraction. It is more difficult to determine what is right than it is to decide what is practical. Moreover, it is possible to have competing notions of justice. It is a subject about which reasonable people can disagree.

Another sample resolution—one which we will discuss at length later in this book— concerns drugs: "Resolved: Soft drugs should be legalized." Again, there is an element of policy here. The legalization of soft drugs, understood here as marijuana, hashish, and other cannabis products, will have a practical impact on a community. As we will see in the model debate that comes in the appendix, practical results can be cited on behalf of both sides in the debate. The affirmative team can argue that, with the decriminalization of marijuana, police forces would be able to focus on more important issues, like violent crime, instead of spending their time trying to halt the traffic in soft drugs. The negative team, however, can argue that the decriminalization of marijuana would lead, naturally, to increased marijuana use—and increased use would lead, in turn, to an increase in other criminal behaviors, since there is a statistical correlation between crime and the use of psychoactive drugs. These, again, are practical matters that would flow from the adoption of a public policy.

There are, however, more abstract ideas that inform this debate. At a higher level, this debate must deal with the conflict between the rights of individuals and the overall good of society. On the one hand, it can be argued that the use of soft drugs is a matter of personal choice. According to this view, the individual should be free to do whatever he or she chooses to do, in the privacy of the home, when the actions involved have no significant impact on others, or on the community at large. The qualification that ends the foregoing sentence is significant. No one would argue that the individual should be free to commit murder within the privacy of the home. Drug use is different, however, because its primary impact is on the individual taking the drugs. On the other hand, a consideration for the overall good of society may support the continued prohibition of soft drugs. Communities, it can be argued, are entitled to establish laws that promote the good of society as a whole, at the expense of personal freedom. When a community requires young people to attend school, for example, it restricts their individual freedom, but the requirement is aimed at benefiting society as a whole. In this view, drug use has a negative impact on society that is demonstrable.

To put it another way, this debate is about the extent of rights. Does the individual have the right to make choices about the conduct of his or her life? Of course—but that right is not absolute. Does a society have the right to create laws that govern the behavior of its citizens? Again, the answer is "yes"—but, again, the right is not absolute. How far do individual rights extend? How far do society's rights extend? And how are we to decide which is greater, when those rights come into conflict? As with our last example, about language and education, these are debatable questions. Reasonable people can disagree about the answers.

CONSTRUCTING RESOLUTIONS

The corollary of this is that constructing a good resolution is a critical part of setting up a good competition and running a debate league. The construction of resolutions is not properly the business of the individual debater, or even of the team. When they enter a competition, the debate resolution has been constructed for them. Coaches, however, are expected to suggest resolutions to league and tournament administrators. Moreover, coaches must offer practice resolutions to the debaters they are training. Accordingly, practitioners of debate should be aware of the characteristics of a good resolution. Conversely, such knowledge will help them to identify the problems that make proposed resolutions weak or unfair.

> **A GOOD RESOLUTION OCCUPIES THE MIDDLE GROUND BETWEEN PURE PRACTICALITY AND PURE ABSTRACTION**

We will begin by restating some of the principles already mentioned above. First, a good resolution, in the Karl Popper format, is one that occupies the middle ground between pure practicality and pure abstraction. That is, it should be about more than the most effective way to spend money, or the most efficient way to achieve a desired result. So, it won't do to argue: "Resolved: The best way to transport goods from Italy to Nepal is through the Suez Canal." In other words, a good resolution must focus on a real conflict between significant values such as liberty or justice. At the same time, the resolution must have some practical dimension. "Resolved: The good life is synonymous with the pursuit of pleasure" might be fun to talk about, but it is too broad and abstract to serve as a resolution for competition.

Along the same lines, a good resolution cannot focus on issues that are primarily religious or personal. For centuries, philosophers have asked, "Does God exist?" The answer to that question, however, is ultimately a matter of personal faith—and as such, not immediately accessible to other people via chains of logic. This question fails as a debate resolution, as it is not susceptible to argument.

Equally, it is a mistake to construct a resolution that requires too much specialized knowledge. It is reasonable, and possible, to debate the legality of abortion. It is another thing to debate whether distinct laws should govern the distribution of abortion drug RU-486, because of possible medical side effects. It is also fair to expect debaters to know something about the nature and use of soft drugs, but it is unreasonable to expect them to know as much about genetically engineered food as someone with a doctorate in biochemistry.

We also emphasized, in earlier discussions, that a debatable proposition is one that has merits on both sides. In other words, a good resolution must be even-handed, and must be constructed in such a way that both sides have something to say. "I believe that the state should act to eliminate the presence of handguns in grammar schools" is the sort of thing politicians sometimes say. Yet this statement makes a poor resolution because there is hardly any way to argue against it. There is simply not much of a negative case. This example may seem obvious, but many debate contests are crippled by resolutions that naturally lean too heavily towards one side or the other.

Take, for example, this resolution, once used in a competition: "Resolved: Dangerous sports should be banned from the school curriculum." It is not too hard to defend such a statement; the corollary is that the negative side has an uphill battle. The word "dangerous" carries a lot of weight. In order to negate the resolution, the negative team has the burden of arguing that danger is a good thing. It would be a more even-handed resolution if it were phrased differently: "Resolved: Students should be allowed to participate in sports which involve the risk of physical injury." The debaters would still have to do some definitional work here—since a physical injury can be anything from a strained muscle to brain damage—but the burdens of argument are more evenly distributed. The main point here is that any proposed resolution must be tested. The people constructing the resolution must sketch out opposing arguments, and be sure that there are good things that can be said both in affirmation and in negation.

THE PRECISE DEFINITION OF TERMS IS AN ESSENTIAL PART OF THE DEBATER'S TASK

Finally, the resolution must not be overly vague or ambiguous. It is perfectly acceptable for the meaning of certain terms to be open; indeed, the precise definition of terms is an essential part of the debater's task. In the resolution about teaching in official languages, for example, the debater must say exactly what is meant by those words. It is not fruitful, however, for the debate resolution to be so open that it can mean almost anything. Another weak resolution, once used in a debate, was this: "Resolved: Parents are too permissive in the 1990s." What parents? Where? About what are they too permissive? The phrase "in the 1990s" limits the question somewhat, but even that limitation is so broad that it adds little meaning to the resolution. Again, such a resolution can be tested. It would be clear enough that this resolution means widely different things to different people. When that is the case, it is hard to imagine that debaters could congregate for a useful exchange of ideas. There is not enough common ground to permit debate.

It takes work to construct a good resolution, but it is not impossible. A perusal of the press shows that contemporary society is a world of perennial controversy. Beneath the controversies that animate the world, a coach will find excellent material for educational debates: the conflict between liberty and order; between personal freedom and social responsibility, between individual rights and the common good, between minority rights and majority rule, between national sovereignty and human rights, between the rule of law and civil disobedience, to cite just a few perennials. Often enough, a resolution can be constructed by looking at a daily newspaper, and analyzing the principles that lie behind the headlines.

GETTING STARTED

In the usual course of operations, the resolution for a debate tournament will be announced a few weeks before the competition by the debate organizers. The resolution is then announced to the debaters by their coach. And then the work begins.

Debate works best as a collaborative activity. When the actual competition takes place, individual debaters will at times be flying solo, even if it's only for three or four minutes, but their flights will not be successful unless they are supported by group preparation with the team. The actual competition is carefully structured and formal. Preparation, however, can be looser and more relaxed. Preparation is a time to let "a hundred flowers bloom and a hundred schools of thought contend," to borrow a phrase from Chairman Mao. It is time to generate ideas, theories, and strategies. It is a time to think creatively, and to test hypotheses. Much of what is generated may be discarded in the end but the parts that endure the test of discussion will be strong. There are many different techniques that can be used to generate and organize ideas. Coaches and teachers typically experiment to see what works best with a given group of individuals. Here are some suggestions:

Brainstorming:

Brainstorming is writing that focuses on process, rather than product. The brainstormer is not supposed to worry about whether the writing on the page is polished, or grammatical, or even spelled correctly. The goal is to write down ideas as they occur, without mental editing. Let's go back to the sample resolution about education in official languages. The teacher would announce the resolution, and ask a student to brainstorm negative ideas. The brainstormer might write "unfair to immigrants," "discriminates against ethnic minorities," "restricts freedom," "homogenizes culture," and a dozen other phrases over the course of five minutes. The phrases are not in any order, or any particular place on the page. A second session would follow for brainstorming positive ideas. When the brainstorming is over, then editing is allowed to start. The debaters are asked to go back over their notes, and to make some judgments. Bad ideas can be crossed out; good ideas can be circled or starred. The debater can use lines and arrows to indicate ideas that are related. They can also use numbers to prioritize ideas—what occurred to them that seemed like the best argument in defense of the resolution?

> BRAINSTORMING IS WRITING THAT FOCUSES ON PROCESS, RATHER THAN PRODUCT

T-Charts, M-Charts and Venn Diagrams:

The T-chart is a more structured method of preparation than brainstorming. Debaters are asked to draw a large letter "T" in their notebooks. On the left side of the vertical, they list positive associations and ideas; on the right side of the vertical, they list negative associations and ideas. The aim is to create complementary pairs: debaters are asked to look for a negative that goes along with a positive. Often, these complementary pairs reflect the classic dichotomies of philosophical thought. One such dichotomy, for example, links the concepts of freedom and order, both of which are regarded as positive values. They are, however, linked in opposition: generally, an increase in personal freedom in a society will produce a decrease in social order. An increase in order will produce a decrease in liberty. An illustration of this tension is the general curfew. If citizens are required to keep off the streets of a city after a certain hour, the city will be more orderly. The freedom of the citizens, however, will be significantly restricted by the curfew. (see page 26)

In any case, it should be remembered that debaters are not preparing to articulate one position in response to the resolution; they will have to argue both sides. The T-chart asks students to start thinking in terms of affirmative and negative cases, and how they relate to each other. When debaters list ideas on a T-chart, they are also asked to think about how those ideas can be countered or refuted.

The M-chart and the Venn Diagram add a third category that falls between positive and negative: neutral ideas about which both sides agree. Take, for example, one of the resolutions that we discussed earlier, the one about education in official languages. Both sides will probably agree that it is the responsibility of the state to provide education for its citizens. Affirmative and negative will disagree about the form of that education, but both will agree that education must be provided. "The state must provide education" is, then, a neutral idea. In physical layout, an M-chart is similar to a T-chart: it simply adds another vertical line, thus creating three columns instead of two. The Venn Diagram is based on circles, rather than columns. In their notebooks, debaters draw two large circles, which overlap slightly. Affirmative ideas go to the far left, and negative ideas go to the far right; common ideas are written in the overlap area.

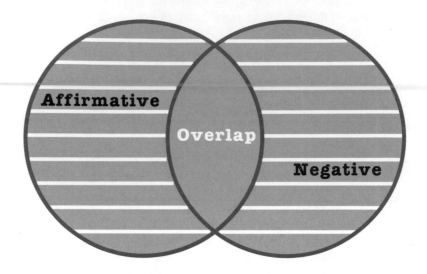

SHARING IDEAS

All of these methods are preliminary; debaters are trying to generate ideas, not to develop a case in finished form. These methods can be used by debaters working individually, or perhaps in pairs, if debaters working alone seem to be completely stuck. The next phase of preparation is a broader sharing of ideas. Debaters can report their findings, while inviting the responses of other debaters; or the teacher may elect to gather all of the ideas, and consolidate them onto one T-chart before beginning discussion. At this point, the discussion should be exploratory, rather than competitive. The teacher running the discussion should encourage debaters to clarify their ideas, to add nuances, or to raise objections. The teacher may also introduce new ideas that have not occurred to the debaters themselves. The debaters, too, should be free to add to the mix of ideas. Ideally, the discussion will suggest new ways of thinking about the resolution.

In the end, the teacher should lead the debaters towards some kind of rough consensus. What do they think are the best arguments in favor of the resolution? What do they think are the best arguments against it? At this point, the arguments will not be complete or fully developed. The goal is to set a general direction, to identify arguments that can be developed with further work.

DEFINING TERMS

In the course of preparation and discussion, it will become clear that, very often, words in the resolution have more than one meaning. Sometimes, the range of possible meanings is fairly limited; sometimes, it is broad, and possible definitions will be radically different. In the latter case, definitions will determine the course of the debate.

An example of a resolution where definitional possibilities are limited may be seen in the model debate that will provide a focus for the next few chapters. The resolution for this debate is: "Resolved: Soft drugs should be legalized." Obviously, it is important to define what is meant by the term "soft drugs." The context of the resolution suggests that these drugs are currently illegal. The resolution, after all, is suggesting that soft drugs are not legal now, and should be made legal. We will discuss the precise meaning of "legalize" in a moment. But there are all kinds of drugs that are illegal in one way or another. A medicine that is not obtainable without a doctor's prescription is not legally available for all to consume. Some medicines are legal in one country, but illegal in another. So it is possible—although it is not very responsible—to argue that the resolution is about cough syrups containing codeine, which are restricted in some countries. It makes more sense,

IT CANNOT BE
ASSUMED THAT A
TERM MEANS
ONLY ONE THING

IT IS THE
RESPONSIBILITY
OF THE
AFFIRMATIVE
TEAM TO DEFINE
KEY TERMS

however, to define soft drugs as psychoactive drugs that have a relatively mild effect. "Soft" is simply a comparative term. The effects of using marijuana are not as drastic as the effects of using heroin, so marijuana is viewed as soft and heroin is referred to as "hard."

We said that it would not be responsible to define soft drugs as a kind of cough remedy, simply because such a definition would not make for a very interesting debate. Most debaters would follow popular usage, and agree to define soft drugs as marijuana and the like. This, however, is the debater's decision. It cannot be assumed that a term means only one thing. As we will see in the model debate, it is the special responsibility of the affirmative team to define key terms. If the words are left undefined, or if there is disagreement over definitions, the negative team is free to impose its own definition.

We promised above to discuss the meaning of legalized. Again, there may not seem to be many possible meanings here. Most people understand the word to mean permitted by law. But it may also mean required by law. With this meaning, the resolution would be saying that the use of soft drugs should be required! Again, such a definition would be possible, but not very responsible. It represents a deliberate twisting of the resolution, presumably to gain strategic advantage. Imagine if the negative team used this disingenuous definition. They would force the affirmative team to defend the concept of mandatory marijuana for all. This sort of sophistry makes a meaningful debate impossible, and should be avoided. If one team arrives at a debate prepared to argue about gun control, understood as the restriction of the sale of firearms, and the other team decides to argue that gun control means skill at handling a weapon, they will not be able to talk to each other.

AS A RESULT
OF DISCUSSIONS
DURING THE
PREPARATION,
DEBATERS
SHOULD ARRIVE
AT A COMMON
UNDERSTANDING
OF TERMS
IN THE
RESOLUTION

To sum up, our resolution concerning the legalization of soft drugs has a fairly narrow range of meanings, but still requires a definition of terms, if only to preclude the possibility of unreasonable definitions. Sometimes, however, the range of reasonable meaning is much broader, and definitions become even more important. Let us look back at another resolution mentioned earlier: "Resolved: The state should provide education only in its official language." Now, what does the term "official language" mean? Does it mean the language used by the government to conduct its own business? Or does it mean the language in common use for other purposes, such as road signs and place names? Or does it mean a language designated by law as the only language acceptable for public transactions in law and business? The United States, for example, has no official language designated by the government, even though the business of government is conducted in English. In the course of discussions, debaters should arrive at a common understanding of what the terms in the resolution mean. Very often, the definitions of terms will directly affect the strategy used to construct a debate case.

Let's look at this resolution in some detail. After each term, we will offer questions and ambiguities that are present; the debaters must decide how to define these terms in a way that is precise and clear, without being fanciful or disingenuous. That is, debaters should not try to twist the words to include meanings that lie outside common usage or common sense.

● **State.** Does this mean a national government only? Or a local government? Can local government have an official language? Or only a national government?

● **Should.** This word implies obligation or necessity. It raises the question: What is the responsibility of the state to its citizens?

● **Provide.** This word means to make available. But how does a state make something available? If a state allows its students freedom to choose schools that do not teach in the official language, is it making those schools available?

● **Education.** What level of education should the state provide? Primary, secondary, post-secondary?

● **Only** means to the exclusion of others. Without this word, the resolution would have a significantly different meaning.

● **In.** This may not seem an important word, but it can be interpreted in significantly different ways. Does the resolution mean that the state should provide instruction in the official language as subject matter? In other words, if the official language is French, should the state provide everyone with the chance to learn the French language? Or does it mean that all instruction should be given in the official language—that math and physics should be taught only in French?

● **Official language.** Some of the ambiguity of this term was suggested above.

In defining terms, a legal (or other specialized) dictionary may be helpful. Certainly, debaters should consult a general comprehensive dictionary in the language used for the resolution. It goes without saying, however, that dictionaries are not final or authoritative. More precisely, dictionaries present a range of possibilities: they show different ways of defining words, but the debaters must choose the definition that seems most reasonable in the context, and which suits them best. The corollary is that dictionaries also provide definitions that are unreasonable and unsuitable in the given context.

> DEBATERS MUST CHOOSE THE DEFINITION THAT SEEMS MOST REASONABLE IN THE CONTEXT

In the chapters that follow, we will be discussing the different kinds of conflict that occur in debate in some detail. For now, we will note that a conflict about definitions is always a possibility. In our model debate, both teams will accept the same understanding of the resolution concerning the legalization of soft drugs, but that kind of agreement is by no means inevitable. Sometimes, the opposing teams will offer conflicting definitions of terms in the resolution. In such cases, part of the debate revolves around who has the more reasonable definition.

Finally, we should note that certain terms that appear in resolutions will invite competing interpretations. When a resolution states that capital punishment is immoral, controversy is inevitable. There are different understandings of the word "immoral" just as there are different understanding of words like "justice" and "ethical." There is no dictionary in the world that can provide a definition that is universally acceptable. But such controversies are part of what gives debate its enduring educational value.

PLANNING NEXT STEPS

All of the foregoing steps will take some time, but they are essential. During the discussions that have taken place, critical thinking has occurred. Debaters have analyzed a problem, and they have begun to take steps to answer it. Before moving on, it is important to stop and assess what has been done, and what remains to be done. Again, it can be helpful to use charts for this process. The teacher can ask the debaters to summarize in their notebooks what has been accomplished. It can be useful for students to identify what they knew before the preparation process started, and to identify what they have learned as a result of the process. A debater may have started, for example, with one understanding of the term "official language" and have learned another during discussion. The most important task at this point, however, is to identify what needs to be done—specifically, what needs to be learned.

For one thing (again, with reference to the model resolution), debaters may recognize that they need to know more about soft drugs, and more about the controversies surrounding legalization. As we suggested earlier, part of the debate is focused on the impact of taking soft drugs, both on the user, and on society as a whole. A debater may have had the thought, for example, that marijuana is really no different, in its effects, from alcohol. True, alcohol is illegal in some parts of the world, but it is, in general, accepted. The debater may be considering an argumentative strategy that marijuana and alcohol are similar, and alcohol is legal; therefore, marijuana should be legal.

In this case, the debater's instincts may be good—but it takes more than instincts to construct an argument. The strategy depends on a presumption: that marijuana and alcohol have similar effects. That presumption has to be turned into a fact. In other words, the debaters must do some research and find out if scientific evidence supports this presumption. They may find, like the negative team in our model debate, that marijuana has effects that are different and significant. It is true that the students are working on a debate, not writing a paper for biology class—but their arguments have to be based on objective reality, not on what they suppose reality to be.

Along the same lines, a debater may make some presumptions about the social effects of marijuana. It seems reasonable to assume that the legalization of marijuana will lead to a significant increase in marijuana use. But economists and historians are fond of citing, somewhat whimsically, the Law of Unintended Consequences. Sometimes, the effect of an action is the opposite of what was anticipated. Take, for example, two policy decisions in the United States. A generation ago, highway speed limits were lowered from 65 miles per hour to 55 miles per hour. It was taken as a given that with lower speeds, there would be fewer highway deaths. That was true; but sociologists were surprised to find that when the speed limits were restored to their former levels, during the past few years, the number of deaths did not go up. Instead, it continued to drop. A similarly well-intentioned act was the decision to raise the legal age for drinking, from 18 to 21, with the intent of curbing underage drinking. Studies have shown, however, that teenage drinking is more widespread than it was when the legal age was lower.

The implications for the debater, perhaps obviously, are similar to what was said above. In order to find out if a reasonable assumption about cause and effect is actually true, the debater must do research. The resolution about the legalization of soft drugs encourages students to follow many avenues of research. Soft drugs have been legalized in some countries and decriminalized in others. It is possible for the student to find out what actually happens when the proposed action is taken. This information can be found in scientific periodicals and policy journals. It also appears, from time to time, in the popular press. Certainly, a cursory search of the Internet will show hundreds of potential sources of information. When they are building a case, it makes sense for members of a team to take on special research assignments. One debater may research the medical effects of marijuana, another may research the link between drug use and crime, a third may explore economic issues. In the end, the fruits of research can be pooled. A successful debate club will usually build a file of articles about public policy issues, which can be augmented as years go by (see below).

Debaters may also determine that they need to know more about particular theories and principles in order to construct their cases. Again, our sample resolution leads us to consider the rights of citizens, as opposed to the rights of the states. A debater who is constructing a case for the legalization of soft drugs may be inclined to argue that, in principle, the rights of the citizens should be presumed paramount. In the classic formulation of the British philosopher, John Stuart Mill, the only justifiable reason for the state to interfere with the individual is to prevent injury to someone else. So the state can act to prevent one citizen from killing another, but it cannot prevent the citizen from harming himself or herself. The point is that Mill's argument is directly relevant to the resolution—if the debater can establish that the drug user affects only himself or herself. Here, then, is another opportunity for research: the debater who is trying to construct an affirmative argument would do well to look at Mill's treatise *On Liberty*, to see how he makes his argument. Especially relevant would be Mill's discussions of drinking and opium, the recreational drug of the 19th century.

DOING RESEARCH It should be remembered that competitive debate is not only (or even primarily) about facts. Debaters are not expected to combat each other with statistical tables and reams of data. Competitive debate is also about the clash of values. When we talk about doing research, then, that definition should be kept in mind. Debaters doing research are not on a fact-finding mission, with the aim of making a report, or recommending an efficient policy. Their aim should be to clarify their understanding of principles, and the interplay of principles and practices. If we affirm the value of bilingual education, it is implicit that we approve of the results that such an education is expected to produce; it makes sense to see what the results are.

Debaters doing research can use a variety of methods. Some debate teams are able to build their own libraries of classic materials; certainly, printed sources abound, and can usually be found in public libraries. Periodicals such as *The Economist* and *The New Republic* regularly focus on domestic and international controversies. The Internet, too, offers many routes of exploration. Some debaters make detailed notes and outlines in their notebooks—this is especially useful for broad arguments (e.g., the libertarian conception of government) that will be relevant to many resolutions. It is also a good idea to make a scrapbook or file of articles.

Finally, many debaters build files of citations: they copy relevant quotations onto index cards for easy use and future reference. We should be clear, however, that debates do not depend upon reference to authority. In other words, debates are supposed to be decided upon the strength of the arguments that the debaters offer. That is not the same as saying that debaters are supposed to act the part of puppeteers, fighting each other with opposing authorities. One side may cite John Stuart Mill; the other side may cite Plato. That doesn't mean the Plato team is right, just because Plato has been around longer and has more titles in paperback. It is also worth remembering, in this context, the remark of Latin debater Cicero, some two thousand years ago: "There is nothing so ridiculous but some philosopher has said it." Now why should we quote Cicero, in the midst of a discussion about the limitations of authority? Simple: Any good writer sometimes likes to quote other writers who have said something particularly well. Debaters should do the same.

MORE GROUP WORK

The preliminary preparation ends, therefore, with the creation of assignments. Debaters leave the group with a clear sense of the research that they need to do before moving on. That research is conducted individually or jointly, but when it is completed, the group reassembles for further discussion. With the fruits of their research, debaters are able to refine their consensus, and to begin mapping out their final cases.

> **WRITTEN OUTLINES MAKE IT EASIER FOR THE COACH TO SEE HOW ARGUMENTS ARE DEVELOPING**

At this point, it is important to start arranging Chairman Mao's "hundred flowers" that have bloomed and this includes reducing the number of flowers! When debaters convene to present their research, they should also come with outlines for their cases. Written outlines make it easier for the coach to see how arguments are developing. Outlines also make it easier for members of a team to share their thoughts and compare strategies. Debate in the Karl Popper format is a team effort. Even though the fundamental outlines of the case will be presented by individuals during the competition itself (see the discussion of the affirmative case and the negative case in following chapters), the construction of the case must be a team effort. The members of the team must argue from a consistent position; their ideas and arguments, as expressed during the competition, must buttress one another. It is essential then, that everyone on the team understand the fundamentals of the team case. That is best achieved if the case is constructed and written by the team as a group effort. For a detailed discussion about the making of the case, see the following chapters.

Chapter 4.
Articulating the Criterion

So far, we have talked about ways to begin thinking about a resolution, preparatory to building an argument. In this chapter, we will talk more precisely about the argument itself. The *criterion*, which we will define below, lies at the center of a good argument. It is the central idea to which all of the points of the argument refer; moreover, it sets the terms on which the argument will be judged.

THE CASE: A FUNCTIONAL OVERVIEW

It may help to begin our discussion by focusing on a specific aspect of competitive debate. At the very heart of the debate is what are called **cases**; each team, affirmative and negative, composes its own case. Cases are presented in speeches called **constructives**. We will discuss each of them in detail in the chapters that follow. Right now, it will suffice to explain their function in the debate. In the constructive speeches, debaters make a case in favor of the resolution or against the resolution. That is, they construct arguments. An argument starts with a position: "I agree (or disagree) with the resolution," or "I think the resolution is true (or false)." But that position must be defended. Why do you agree? The debater must answer that question with a series of statements. In one way or another, the debate must say, "I agree with the resolution because of *x*, and because of *y*, and because of *z*." In short, the debater must support his or her position with arguments.

THE CONFLICT OF VALUES AND THE CRITERION

Throughout this handbook, we have emphasized the nature of the conflict in debate: it is, we have said, a conflict between principles. We have also called it a conflict between values. At this point, we should take some time to examine what those words mean. **Values** and **principles** are related to the concept of the good. When we value something, we are acknowledging it as a good. It may be a state that it is good to achieve; an action that it is good to do; an ideal for which it is good to strive. A principle is a guide to good actions. When we say that we follow certain principles, we mean that we are, in our judgment, doing something that is good or right.

> **THE NATURE OF THE CONFLICT IN DEBATE IS BETWEEN VALUES AND PRINCIPLES**

People have many values, ranging from the mundane to the exalted. We may say we value a good night's sleep, and we also value making personal sacrifices for the sake of the community. In other words, the average person holds more than one value, and there is nothing illogical or inconsistent about that. And yet, values must be placed in a hierarchy. When values conflict, the individual must choose which value is most important. Say, for example, that your best friend has stolen something from a store, and the shopkeeper asks you if you know something about it. You value loyalty to your friend, but you also value telling the truth. You must decide which is the higher value. Conflicts of value are common; we must often decide between individual liberty and the common good, or between majority rule and minority rights.

In constructing a debate argument, it is necessary to have a clear sense of which primary value is being upheld by the argument. To return to the framework outlined above: one way or another, the debater must say "I agree with the resolution because..." What follows is the **criterion**: "...because I believe that the highest good in this context is *x*, and the affirmation of this resolution will maximize *x*." That value, or highest good, can be many things. It can be individual liberty, or social order, or the common good, or the rule of law, or justice, or the general well-being of the population. Different values are relevant to different contexts and different resolutions.

So this is really the most important task for any team constructing a case. They must identify and define the primary value, or criterion. In their initial discussions of the resolution, team members will often consider the importance of a number of different values. Say, for example, that the resolution is about the morality of abortion. While planning their strategy, the team arguing in favor of legalized abortion may consider the value of majority rule. If majority rule is the highest value, and most people in a society favor abortion, then legalized abortion upholds that value. But they may also consider the value of personal freedom: If the individual should be free to act without interference from the state, and abortion is conceived of as a personal matter, then legalized abortion upholds personal freedom. There are, of course, multiple values to be considered on the opposing side. The team must decide, in plotting its strategy, which value is most important in the context of the resolution and can be supported by the strongest arguments.

In the process of selecting an appropriate criterion around which to construct their cases, members of the team will, naturally, develop a list of reasons why the criterion they choose is the most important. These reasons will not necessarily become parts of the debate itself—but they may be. Say, for example, that a team determines that "justice" is the most important value. In presenting their case, the debaters must explicitly state that justice is the most important value, and that they believe it should serve as the criterion for judging the debate. They are not required as a matter of course, however, to present their reasons for choosing justice, nor to say why it is more important than the common good. It very often happens, however, that the opposing team will explicitly challenge the criterion chosen; the negative team, for example, can say that they think that justice is not relevant or important in the context of the resolution (and they will, accordingly, offer their own criterion). When such a challenge is presented, the team must be prepared to defend their original choice. Everyone on the team, therefore, must go into the competition with a clear understanding of why the criterion was chosen.

We have used the terms "criterion" and "value" interchangeably in the foregoing discussion. It should be clear, by now, what we mean by the word "value". As described above, a value is something that we believe to be good. The word "criterion" indicates how a value functions during a debate. A criterion, in ordinary usage, is a standard by which something is judged. One criterion for judging an ice skater is the height of her jumps; a tenor is judged, in part, by the criterion of his vocal range. In the context of debate, the criterion is the standard by which (according to the debater) the debate should be judged. When she articulates her criterion, the debater is saying, in effect, that her team should be judged on two things: first, their success in showing that their value is more important and second, their success in demonstrating that affirming (or negating) the resolution will uphold that value. If the criterion of the affirmative team is justice, all of the arguments offered by the team must show how justice is either maintained or promoted by the affirmation of the resolution. If the criterion of the negative team is personal freedom, all of the arguments offered by the team must show how personal freedom is either maintained or promoted by the negation of the resolution.

SOME CONSIDERATIONS REGARDING CRITERIA

For a case to be successful, it is essential for the debater to have a clear understanding of the criterion offered. This is especially important when using terms such as "justice"—justice has been defined in radically different ways by different thinkers. Justice may mean, for example, punishing those who break the law; or it may mean giving each person his due; or it may mean, as Socrates argues in *The Republic*, fulfilling one's natural obligations. The debater must be able to define her criterion precisely.

It is also important to recognize that value conflicts must be taken in the context of the resolution. To put it another way, values are rarely absolute. We might say, as a general principle, that the right to privacy is more important than public security. When we say that, we affirm that the government should not have the right to search private homes routinely, simply because such searches *might* uncover threats to public security. In that conflict between privacy and security, the right to privacy is more important. But in other contexts, we may decide differently. After all, a metal detector in an airport represents an invasion of privacy for the sake of public security. In that context, however, we might say that the invasion is not significant, and should be outweighed by concern for public safety. The point here is that debaters must defend a given criterion within the context of the resolution, not as an abstract, absolute philosophical belief.

Finally, it must be emphasized that the criteria should be fair and relevant. There is a temptation, in debate, to look for positions that are untouchable, rather than defensible. One tactic is to construe the resolution in a way that goes outside its commonly understood context. Take, for example, the resolution we mentioned earlier, regarding the question of the state's responsibility to provide education only in its official language. Most people would construe that to mean there are two alternatives: either the state should teach in one language, or else it should teach in more than one language. The creatively perverse team, however, could find a third alternative by taking an extreme libertarian position: viz., no language! That is, this team could argue that the resolution should be negated because the state should not be teaching anything at all, in any language—because the state should not be involved in education. The debaters would argue for the value of having the smallest possible government. Yes, it's possible, logically, to take such a position—but it ignores the implication in the resolution that the debate is supposed to be about the use of official languages, not about whether there should be such a thing as state education in the first place. The problem with this tactic, ultimately, is that it makes debate impossible. Affirmative and negative are not able to meet on any common ground. One team has prepared to discuss the respective value of competing alternatives; the other team—the whimsical libertarians—arrives with the intention of arguing that both alternatives are unacceptable. The perverse criterion isn't really fair.

It is equally unfair to offer vague and sweeping criteria. If the affirmative debater says that he is upholding the criterion of truth, or goodness, the negative side can hardly argue for a competing value. Again, the debater who uses such broad formulations is trying to build a position that is out of his opponent's reach.

The importance of relevance can be understood in a similar way. Sometimes, it seems clever to articulate criteria that are easily measured, because they seem inarguable. Money, for example, is easily measured, but a debater may decide to use it as a criterion for situations where it is irrelevant. Say, for example, the resolution concerns the justification for capital punishment. It is quite possible, of course, to calculate the costs of public executions, and to compare those costs with the higher net cost of keeping inmates in jail, and so conclude that capital punishment is cost-effective. With this criterion in mind, the debater argues that reduction in government expenses is a good. This is hardly a relevant criterion, however, when the resolution raises questions about moral rights and duties. Such a criterion is reminiscent of Jonathan Swift's classic satire, *A Modest Proposal,* in which he argues that the best solution to overpopulation and starvation in Ireland is for the poor to sell their babies for food. This, he notes, will be good for the restaurant business as well! Cost may seem inarguable, but the argument that includes it in this context is substantively weak.

LEVELS OF CONFLICT IN A DEBATE We will discuss conflict at greater length in subsequent chapters, but for now, we should note that conflict in debate occurs on different levels. Affirmative and negative can disagree at the highest level, the level of criteria, but it should be noted that affirmative and negative sides do not necessarily have to have distinct and competing criteria. Say, for example, that the resolution concerns the legalization of narcotic drugs. Both sides could say, reasonably, that their primary value is public safety, and the reduction of crime. The side arguing against legalization could argue that narcotics users frequently commit crimes while under the influence of drugs; that narcotics users are often unable to hold jobs and resort to crime in order to acquire drugs, and so on. The side arguing for legalization, however, could argue that the restriction of drugs actually creates a criminal subculture; since drug use can never be eradicated, there will always be a system—whether legal or illegal—to supply drugs to users. Therefore, it would be better for the

> IT IS UNFAIR TO OFFER VAGUE AND SWEEPING CRITERIA
>
> THE CRITERIA SHOULD BE FAIR AND RELEVANT

state to control distribution, and to render the criminal suppliers unnecessary. The conflict here is not about the criterion itself, but about the best way to maximize the value.

BUILDING AN ARGUMENT: THE IMPORTANCE OF COHERENCE AND RELEVANCE

In the foregoing discussion, we have touched on the substance of the argument that follows the criterion. The debater is expected to offer a series of reasons for her position. She must say why her position will maximize or foster or uphold the value she has articulated. (It does not matter whether she is arguing affirmative or negative; in the first case, she argues why affirming the resolution will uphold the value; in the second case, she argues why negating the resolution will uphold the value.)

All of the reasons must relate back to the primary value. In other words, they must be relevant. Debaters must resist the temptation to multiply the benefits of their position, or they will sound like the aforementioned *Modest Proposal*—which offers a panacea, a solution that is good for any problem that can be imagined, from indigestion to inflation. The reasons, or arguments, should be designed to prove one larger thesis.

We will look closely at a constructive speech, which articulates a case, in Chapter Seven. But before examining a specific case, we will discuss some of the practical concerns involved in writing cases, and we will examine some strategies of argumentation.

Chapter 5.
Writing the Case and Planning Strategy

So far, we have focused on two essential parts of preparation: debate teams must begin by coming to an understanding of the resolution, and then they must decide what criterion will be most appropriate for their case. In this chapter, we will discuss the remaining steps that must be taken before competition begins. The debaters must write their cases in final form, and test them, as opponents would test them. And they must develop general strategies of defense and refutation.

WRITING THE CASE

In Chapter Two, we touched briefly on the nature of the constructive speech. In the constructives, debaters lay out their arguments in full. That is, they offer an understanding of the terms in the resolution, they articulate a criterion, and they offer reasons in support of their position. This complete argument is called the case. At the risk of belaboring the point: the constructive speech presents the case.

> **DEBATERS LAY OUT THEIR ARGUMENTS IN FULL IN THE CONSTRUCTIVE SPEECHES**

For competition, of course, every team needs two complete cases, one affirming the resolution, and one negating it, since they will need to do both things in the course of the contest. Generally, teams should work together to compose their cases, revising and editing drafts collaboratively. In competition, many debaters prefer not to read aloud the final text as it has been written out; instead, they like to speak less formally, using notes. Nonetheless, the case should be written out in full beforehand: this allows for true collaboration by the members of the team. The case must be the product of united minds; unless each member of the team understands the case personally and deeply, good teamwork during the competition will be impossible.

The affirmative constructive comes first when the debate round begins; debaters are free, therefore, to give the entire allotted time to prepared remarks. The negative constructive, however, comes third in the sequence of sections, after the affirmative constructive and an initial section of cross-examination. Accordingly, the negative constructive is coupled with a rebuttal. The negative debater will present his own case against the resolution, but will also respond to the arguments that have been offered by the affirmative side. The prepared negative constructive, then, is shorter than the prepared affirmative constructive. The negative debater does not use the full six minutes allotted to this section for the constructive; his prepared remarks should last only about three minutes, leaving three minutes for rebuttal. (The division of this section is made at the discretion of the negative debater. No formal time is stipulated in the Popper format.)

ANTICIPATING OBJECTIONS

Good debaters must be able to think on their feet. The constructive arguments that are written out beforehand constitute only a small fraction of the debate. Most of what is said during a debate round is spontaneous. The affirmative team doesn't know what the negative case is going to be like until they hear it in the round. The negative team, of course, is equally ignorant of the affirmative case.

Nevertheless, it is a good idea to make reasonable guesses about what might be said when the debate begins. There are multiple dimensions to this task. First, the debaters must examine their affirmative case, and ask themselves what objections may be raised against their arguments. They may claim, for example, that legalizing marijuana will increase crime, since people under the influence of marijuana commit many crimes. What might the negative side say about that contention? Perhaps the negative team will say that people under the influence of alcohol also commit many crimes—but that the prohibition of alcohol does not eliminate crime. The incidence of crime is unrelated to the availability of alcohol, and would also be unrelated to the availability of drugs. Or maybe the negative team will use the alcohol parallel in a different way: people under the influence of alcohol commit many crimes, but most people who drink do not commit crimes. Indeed, most marijuana users do not commit crimes (other than the crime involved in purchasing an illegal drug). There is no reason to think that legalization will change the proportion of criminals and non-criminals in the pool of marijuana users.

The affirmative team does not know, of course, which of these objections the negative team will raise—or if negative will raise an objection that they haven't even imagined. But it is wise for them to prepare a response beforehand. In competition, they will have to rebut the refutation; their response will usually be better if they have thought about it before the debate.

Of course, every team has to argue both sides of the resolution during competition, so this kind of preparation must be done twice: debaters must think of possible objections to their affirmative case, and they must think of possible objections to their negative case. Finally, they should imagine cases that might be constructed by an opponent, and think of objections that they would be able to make.

Now, this may seem like redundant and unnecessary labor: after all, if the debaters are constructing arguments for both sides, it may seem like they are automatically drafting objections to their own cases. But that is not necessarily so, if only because there is more than one good way to construct an argument for each side; not every possible objection to their affirmative case is going to be contained in their negative case. Let's say, for example, that a team has constructed an affirmative case in favor of the legalization of marijuana; they argue, in essence, that marijuana should be legalized because no one is harmed by the use of the drug other than the people who use it. (They have articulated personal liberty as their criterion.) Now, they may imagine that the opposing team may argue, in a debate, that marijuana use does hurt other people, because marijuana users commit crimes. They themselves think that this is not a particularly good argument, and they have not put anything like it into their own negative case. And yet, they must consider it, and plan a response. In other words, they have to plan to respond to arguments that they would never make themselves. They have to go beyond the arguments that were incorporated into their own cases. In this imaginary scenario, they might respond that crimes are also committed by people under the influence of alcohol—which means it is a logical corollary of the opposing position that alcohol should be illegal, too. Needless to say, they are preparing this point in case this objection is raised. No sane debater would include the point that marijuana users commit no more crimes than alcohol users as part of the original case.

Along the same lines, they must conceive of potential cases to be made by their opponents. Let's say that their negative case is founded on the criterion of national sovereignty—but they know, from their own discussions, that a negative case could have been founded on the criterion of majority rule. Before the competition, debaters have to build that possibility into an imaginary scenario: "What if they argue a case based on majority rule? What arguments will they be likely to make? How can we refute them?"

THE VALUE OF ROLE-PLAYING In modern politics, the exercise of role-playing has become a common tool. A politician is scheduled, for instance, to hold a press conference about a vital issue; it is common for his staff to prepare him by asking the toughest questions that a journalist might come up with. The interplay between politician and staff is not hypothetical: e.g., "What will you say if someone asks about how you will handle potential cost overruns?" Instead, staff members act out parts in an improvised play: "Sir, your last proposal regarding education cost three times the original estimate, and ended up costing taxpayers millions of euros. What are you doing to make sure that the same thing doesn't happen with this proposal?" Role-playing is also used to prepare candidates for public office for debates. Every candidate knows he has vulnerabilities that will probably be exploited by an opponent; in this case, staff members play the role of opponent making hostile remarks (e.g., "You promised an ethical administration, but two members of your advisory council have been investigated for criminal violations of the law.") The goal of role-playing is, perhaps, obvious: if the anticipated objection or question emerges in a real situation, the politician will already have had practice responding to it.

Before a debate, role-playing can have a similar function. Team members can prepare each other by assuming the roles of their opponents in practice sessions. It isn't necessary to conduct a full-length debate, with all its appointed parts; even a few rounds of cross-examination or rebuttal will help the debater to get ready for the real event.

PLOTTING STRATEGIES FOR CROSS-EXAMINATION

We will discuss cross-examination more fully in Chapter Eight. Much of cross-examination is reactive; that is, the debaters formulate their questions in response to what their opponents have said. But cross-examination can also be preemptive: that is, debaters use questions to gain concessions from their opponents—concessions that may be valuable for supporting their own case.

To give just a brief example: Let's say that the negative team has written a case that supports the criterion of personal liberty. Even before they present their case, in the negative constructive speech, they have the chance to ask questions of the affirmative team during the initial round of cross-examination. This cross-examination represents an opportunity to gain concessions; it will help the negative case if they can get the affirmative debater to agree that the government has the right to restrict individual liberty only in certain cases, and for valid reasons. In the speech that follows the cross-examination, the negative speaker can build on that concession: "Our opponents agree that the government's right to restrict liberty is limited, and we will say why in our case..."

The point here is that the preemptive part of cross-examination should be planned before the competition. When the round is underway, the actual cross-examination may head in another direction; nonetheless, it is wise to plot a strategy that may be of use when the time comes.

PRACTICING FLOW

There is one more kind of preparation worth discussing. It is essential to practice note-taking skills. In competition, the progress of the debate, from point to point, through the sequences of arguments, and questions and rebuttals, is called the flow of the debate. The verb form—to flow the debate—means to record the debate as it goes along. After all, debate does not consist of the presentation of static speeches; it is, rather, characterized by responses, by the back-and-forth exchange of ideas and arguments. A debater cannot succeed unless he listens carefully to what his opponent says, and responds to it. In the world of competitive debate, the axiomatic principle is that "silence means consent." If one team makes an argument, and their opponents do not attempt to answer it, or refute it, it is assumed that the opponents agree with the contention. (To put it another way, it is assumed that they do not answer it because they find it unanswerable.) Therefore, it is critically important for debaters to keep track of what their opponents have said (and to keep track of their own responses). This is not, we should emphasize, a specialized responsibility, assigned to one member of the team; rather, every member of the team should flow the debate. This allows the preparation time during the debate—when responses are planned—to be used with far greater efficiency.

> A DEBATER CANNOT SUCCEED UNLESS HE LISTENS AND FLOWS CAREFULLY

Most debaters create flow charts on sheets of paper in a pad. The page is divided vertically into columns, each column corresponding to a section of the debate. Most debaters will use two sheets to cover one round. In each column, the debater notes, in outline form, the points made in each section. Horizontal lines and arrows can be used to connect contentions with refutations. Both debaters and judges should flow at least the criterion and the numbered arguments. (In the appendix, we have included a sample flow chart.)

During practices, debaters should form the habit of recording the flow of debates to which they listen. In this setting, of course, it is possible to check flow charts for accuracy and completeness. When in competition, debaters will be better able to reason and respond if they have practiced this skill beforehand.

T-CHART

POSITIVE ASSOCIATIONS | **NEGATIVE ASSOCIATIONS**

M-CHART

POSITIVE ASSOCIATIONS | **NEUTRAL ASSOCIATIONS** | **NEGATIVE ASSOCIATIONS**

FLOW CHART

1A FIRST AFFIRMATIVE	1N FIRST NEGATIVE	2A SECOND AFFIRMATIVE	2N SECOND NEGATIVE	3A THIRD AFFIRMATIVE	3N THIRD NEGATIVE

Chapter 6.
Logical Strategies and Logical Errors

There are countless ways to build an argument, and we cannot hope to describe them all in a book of this size. But we will describe some ways of thinking about an argument, and we will offer a compendium of logical errors. We should say, at the outset, that this description is not intended to serve as a recipe for the construction of a case. It isn't possible to look at a resolution and say, "Now we will build a case, using two arguments by analogy, and one argument by example." Nonetheless, this discussion will have value as an analytical tool. It should help debaters test the strength of arguments they are considering, as they build their cases. And it should also help debaters understand the vulnerabilities of arguments offered by their opponents during a debate.

DEDUCTION AND INDUCTION IN DEBATE

In formal logic, a distinction is made between deduction and induction. The distinction between induction and deduction, and the model of the syllogism, can be traced back more than two thousand years to the Greek philosopher Aristotle. In deduction, the reasoner draws a particular conclusion from general truths.

This is a classic syllogism — that is, a three-step deductive argument:

1 ALL MEN ARE MORTAL (PREMISE) + 2 SOCRATES IS A MAN (PREMISE) THEREFORE 3 SOCRATES IS MORTAL (CONCLUSION)

The first two statements in this series are called premises. If both of them are true, then the third statement—the conclusion—must also be true. This process of logic is used, quite commonly, in mathematics. Take, for example, a simple geometrical proof. If we are told that each of two angles in a triangle measures 60 degrees and we know that a triangles have 180 degrees, then we also know that the third angle measures 60 degrees, and we can conclude that the triangle in question is equilateral. This conclusion is logically inevitable, given our definition of triangles.

Induction, however, moves in the opposite logical direction. It begins with particular truths, and attempts to draw a more general conclusion. Suppose that we want to prove that Socrates is a man. It isn't enough simply to say that "all men are mortal, and Socrates is mortal." Those statements may be true, but they do not lead to our desired conclusion. Why? Because there are other things, besides men, that are mortal. Dogs are mortal—so if all we know is that Socrates is mortal, then Socrates may be a dog, not a man.

But suppose we start multiplying our statements. We already know that Socrates is mortal. Let's say that Socrates also speaks Greek, teaches philosophy in a university, smokes a pipe, and has a bank account. It does not necessarily follow that Socrates is a man, but it would be reasonable for us to conclude that he is. Why doesn't it necessarily follow? Socrates might be a woman.

This example illustrates the logical method of induction, which is used widely in everyday life. Induction is, for example, the method used by most doctors in making a medical diagnosis. A doctor knows, for example, that the streptococcus bacillus makes throats red and that it sometimes creates white spots in the throat. He also knows that infected patients are likely to have a high fever and to feel pain when swallowing. Now, let's say that a doctor examines a patient who is a student in a school where there has been a widespread occurrence of strep throat, and he discovers all of these symptoms. None of them is conclusive independently—there are other illnesses that cause sore throat and fever, and one of those other illnesses could be affecting the patient. But when he takes all of the symptoms together, he makes a reasonable conclusion based on them. He concludes that the patient has strep throat, and either begins treating it, or orders a test to confirm his diagnosis before treatment.

Both of these methods of argument will be used in debate. Let's say, for example, that the resolution is about the morality of capital punishment. A deductive argument might run as described below.

DEDUCTIVE ARGUMENT:

1. It is morally wrong to kill any individual who is unarmed and not actively engaged in harming others (MAJOR PREMISE)

+

2. Prisoners who are executed are unarmed, and incapable of harming others (MINOR PREMISE)

THEREFORE

3. IT IS MORALLY WRONG TO EXECUTE PRISONERS (CONCLUSION)

We can illustrate an inductive argument by considering a proposal to decriminalize narcotics and to make them available under medical supervision. The debater might argue according to the chart below. With all of these reasons, the debater would conclude that it would be good to decriminalize narcotics.

INDUCTIVE ARGUMENT:

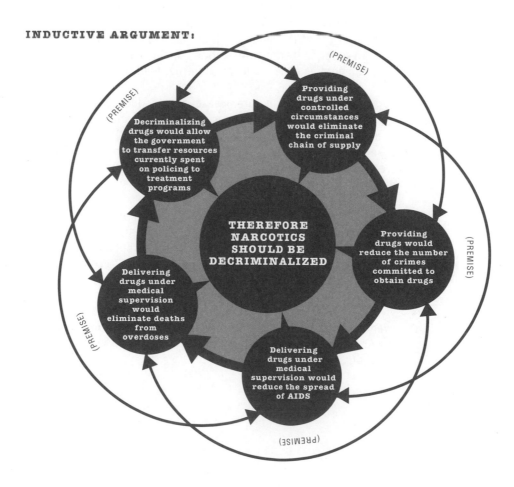

(PREMISE) Decriminalizing drugs would allow the government to transfer resources currently spent on policing to treatment programs

(PREMISE) Providing drugs under controlled circumstances would eliminate the criminal chain of supply

(PREMISE) Providing drugs would reduce the number of crimes committed to obtain drugs

(PREMISE) Delivering drugs under medical supervision would reduce the spread of AIDS

(PREMISE) Delivering drugs under medical supervision would eliminate deaths from overdoses

THEREFORE NARCOTICS SHOULD BE DECRIMINALIZED

We should note that most of the arguments encountered in debate are inductive, rather than deductive. Deductive arguments work best when they are founded on absolute statements: e.g., the angles in a triangle add up to 180 degrees. In social spheres, absolute statements are hard to come by.

WEAKNESSES IN DEDUCTIVE AND INDUCTIVE ARGUMENTS

Deductive arguments are inherently strong. If the premises are true, then the conclusion must be true. In order to disprove the conclusion, then, one must refute the truth of one of the premises. Consider this syllogism, which corresponds to Aristotle's thinking about families, as outlined in his Politics:

DEDUCTIVE ARGUMENT:

1 The most capable family member should rule the family unit (MAJOR PREMISE) + 2 Men are more capable than women (MINOR PREMISE) THEREFORE 3 THE HUSBAND SHOULD RULE THE FAMILY UNIT (CONCLUSION)

The conclusion is perfectly logical—but many of us would object to the premises. It is not necessarily true that only one person should rule the family unit. It is certainly not true that men are more capable than women are. Even the word "capable" is vague. What particular skill or talent is it meant to indicate? We have more than one weak point to probe here. In order to disprove Aristotle's conclusion, we need to disprove one of his first two statements; if either of them is untrue, then the argument is not valid.

Inductive arguments are, by nature, weaker than deductive arguments—we indicated that much in our discussion above. A series of statements may lead us to conclude that Socrates is a man, when Socrates is actually a woman. The doctor may reasonably conclude, based on the symptoms, that the patient has strep throat. But the patient may, in fact, have a blood disorder that produces those symptoms. The problem with inductive arguments is that they are always incomplete.

We might have come to a very different conclusion about Socrates' sex if we had more facts. The doctor might have made a different diagnosis if he had seen a blood analysis. The debater arguing in favor of the legalization of narcotics came to his conclusion based on the results of decriminalization that he thought probable. He did not consider other probable results.

A MODERN LOGICAL MODEL

In the twentieth century, the British philosopher Stephen Toulmin developed a model similar to Aristotle's, but distinctly different in significant ways. We can start by looking at a simple logical chain.

(MAJOR PREMISE)   (MINOR PREMISE)   (CONCLUSION)

As noted, according to the Aristotelian approach, if the premises above are true, the conclusion must be true. But Toulmin argues that there is a flaw in the premises that may not be evident in the form. The first premise is a kind of universal law, a statement that is taken as true in all circumstances. The second premise is not a law. It is a piece of evidence. As we know from our earlier discussion, both of these premises may be untrue: the smoke from a smoke machine is not produced by fire; and the speaker may think he sees smoke, but it may be fog.

To Toulmin's thinking, the syllogism is not as objective as it appears. The problem is that it may be sneaking assumptions past the listener, who does not focus on the vulnerability of the premises. The problem is made worse when the syllogism is not about physical facts, but about values. Let's revisit the syllogism that we offered earlier, about capital punishment.

A SIMPLE SYLLOGISM:

(MAJOR PREMISE)   (MINOR PREMISE)   (CONCLUSION)

As it stands, this syllogism seems untouchable. The conclusion follows logically from the premises, and ends the argument. Toulmin, however, argues that the labels and the sequence of the classic syllogism do not accurately reflect what is going on. The conclusion, he says, is really a starting point, not an ending point. The final term of the syllogism above is really a claim, not a conclusion. It is something that the speaker wants to prove. In order to prove it, the speaker must articulate what Toulmin calls a warrant. The warrant can be understood as an underlying principle, as the idea that connects the claim with its support, the grounds of the argument. Toulmin emphasizes that the warrant itself must be established and cannot be taken as given. That, he feels, is what happens when the reasoner uses Aristotle's seemingly neutral, objective terms, "major premise" and "minor premise." Toulmin argues that the premises themselves need to be established. For example, it is not a self-evident truth that it is morally wrong to kill any individual who is unarmed and not actively engaged in harming others. That is something that the speaker thinks, and it may be something with which his listeners agree, but it remains a debatable proposition.

In Toulmin's model, our sample syllogism would look something like the following chart. Toulmin's terms are meant to emphasize that the reasoner has much to prove. The warrant itself is an arguable position. The support, too, must be proven. As in the classic syllogism, the terms are interdependent. In the classic syllogism, one can disprove the conclusion by disproving one of the premises. In Toulmin's model, the claim cannot be proven if the warrant is not proven, and the grounds are not proven.

TOULMIN'S MODEL:

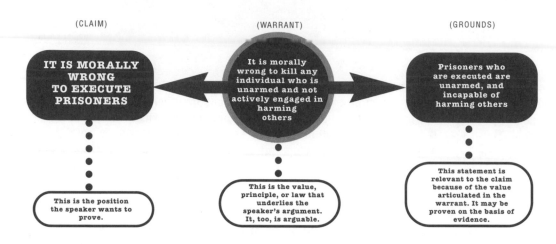

As may be evident, this model is compatible with the terms we have offered in this book. The claim corresponds to the debater's position, either in favor of or against the resolution. The warrant corresponds to the criterion. The grounds correspond to the arguments, or the evidence supplied by the speaker.

By including these models as part of our chapter, we do not mean to introduce a set of terms or jargon as part of competitive debate. Debaters should not have to worry about labeling parts of their arguments as major premises or warrants. They do not have to announce whether they are being inductive or deductive. These models should, however, help debaters to understand how the parts of an argument fit together. With such an understanding, they will be better able to understand how to construct arguments, and how to refute them.

ARGUMENTATIVE STRATEGIES

Deduction and induction are types of logic; as such, they are used in various arguments. Now, we will consider some larger argumentative strategies. These are ways of constructing an argument. Each of the strategies outlined below may make use of deduction or induction along the way. Indeed, many arguments will use both types of logic, and often, a deductive syllogism is built upon a premise that is the product of inductive reasoning. In effect, that makes the entire argument inductive.

Arguments by analogy: An analogy is a comparison, which focuses on the similarity of two different things. The logical structure runs like this: A and B are similar. Therefore, if something is true about A, then it is also true about B. Sometimes, the purpose of the analogy is to illuminate a problem by comparing it to something that is easily understood. In his novel *War and Peace*, Tolstoy offers a famous analogy to explain the principle of historical causation. An ignorant man, he writes, will look at a locomotive and wonder how it moves. He will conclude that it moves because of the will of the engineer. That conclusion, of course, is erroneous. Tolstoy argues that it is just like the conclusion made by historians who think that great men shape historical events. Those great men do not make nations move, any more than the engineer makes a locomotive move. Obviously, the reader will agree with Tolstoy that the man who thinks that the engineer moves the train is mistaken. The success of the analogy depends on whether the reader thinks that it makes sense to compare history to a locomotive.

Analogies will frequently be used in competitive debate. Typically, a controversial situation will be compared to a non-controversial situation. The debater hopes that the listener will come to the same conclusion about both. Say, for example, that the resolution concerns the legalization of marijuana. A debater may argue that marijuana is like alcohol. He presumes that his listener finds no difficulty with the legality of alcohol. If it is acceptable to permit alcohol, he argues, why should it be unacceptable to permit marijuana, when they are so much alike? He may even extend the comparison to argue that the legal prohibition of alcohol in America, during the 1920s, had disastrous effects on law and order, and that the current prohibition of marijuana has an equally deleterious effect.

We should note that there is a difference between the two examples discussed above. Tolstoy's analogy is figurative. History is like a train only to an imaginative mind. The comparison between alcohol and marijuana is literal. There are objective similarities between the two substances.

Weaknesses of arguments by analogy: Analogies are frequently persuasive, and rhetorically effective. They are always vulnerable, however, because they depend upon a comparison that can be disputed. Let's look at the alcohol-marijuana analogy in the form of a syllogism:

A SIMPLE SYLLOGISM:

The syllogism is not logically sound, because marijuana is not contained in the major premise. In contrast, it would be right if the syllogism were about vodka. It is wrong to prohibit alcohol; vodka is alcohol; therefore, it is wrong to prohibit vodka. Moreover, as in any syllogism, the conclusion depends on the validity of minor premise, that marijuana is like alcohol. In some ways it is, but in some ways it isn't. In order to refute the argument, the debater's opponent needs simply to say why marijuana isn't like alcohol. If the minor premise is refuted, then the conclusion will not stand.

If we use Toulmin's model here, it highlights the fragility of the above conclusion:

TOULMIN'S MODEL:

We will close by noting that the figurative analogy is easier to dismiss than the literal analogy: It's Impossible to prove that history is just like a locomotive. If the comparison is dismissed as absurd, the argument falls apart.

Arguments from examples: An argument from examples depends heavily on the inductive method of logic. With this strategy, the debater offers evidence of what is known and inarguable. She presumes that the same conclusions can be drawn about the unknown. Again, let's say that the debate is about the legalization of marijuana. The debater would introduce, as evidence, the examples of countries that had legalized marijuana. In every case, she would argue, the legalization of the drug led to no increase in crime or other negative social effects. Moreover, in every case, the law enforcement agencies were able to reduce their expenses, and concentrate their resources on other needs. She would conclude, then, that the examples show that the legalization of marijuana is a good thing, as a general principle. As a corollary, it would be good to legalize marijuana in every country.

This strategy is similar, in some ways, to the argument based on analogy, because there is a kind of comparison being made. If this action had a certain effect in Situation A and Situation B and Situation C, then we can conclude that the same thing will happen in Situation D. Of course, the comparison is also broader than in a simple analogy, which usually has only two terms of comparison. But the argument from examples is different. An analogy makes a comparison between things that are dissimilar, as well as similar. Alcohol and marijuana are not the same thing. They belong to different classes. Examples, however, are seen as individual items within one class. In a sense, this strategy aspires to articulate a general law that applies in any particular situation, based on the evidence of what is already known. The scientific method is, in essence, founded on an argument from examples. If an experiment can be repeated with the same result in a finite number of tries, we assume that the same result will occur in an infinite number of tries.

Weaknesses of arguments from examples: An argument from examples has the inherent weakness of any inductive argument. It depends on a limited and finite number of examples. The debater who uses examples that show good effects to support the legalization of marijuana can be countered by an opponent who offers examples that show bad effects. A large number of examples may be persuasive, but examples themselves do not constitute immutable laws.

THE MAIN WEAKNESS OF AN ARGUMENT FROM EXAMPLES IS ITS DEPENDENCY ON A LIMITED NUMBER OF EXAMPLES

An argument based on examples is also vulnerable because of the element of comparison that it contains. Let's say, for the sake of argument, that all of the countries where marijuana has been successfully legalized have small populations and low crime rates; moreover, studies show that marijuana is used by only five percent of the population. It could be argued, in opposition, that the situation is completely different in a large country with a high crime rate, where marijuana is already used illegally by 20 percent of the population. In other words, it could be argued that the law that is putatively established by the examples is not universal, and will not apply in a situation that is significantly different. It is worth observing, in this context, that there seem to be few universal laws that govern human behavior the way that laws govern the world of physics or chemistry.

Arguments of cause and effect: The strongest logical arguments do not depend on the introduction of extraneous evidence, either by analogy or from examples. These arguments depend, instead, upon an analysis of cause and effect. The principle of cause and effect, of course, is central to the scientific method that is used in the physical sciences. In the sphere of social sciences, cause and effect is not usually as clear as it might be in a physics laboratory; nonetheless, the principle continues to operate.

Let's take a simple example. A state education system does not require the study of laboratory science in secondary school. There have been a declining number of students pursuing technical degrees in college, and there is also a national shortage of engineers. It is clear enough that the last two facts are related. If there are fewer students doing technical degrees, the logical result would be fewer engineers. Unless demand for engineers also fell, the result would be a shortage. Here, we can see the cause of the effect clearly. But we might also extend the causal line back further to consider the lack of science requirements in secondary school. Science is not required, but 50 percent of the students choose to study it anyway. A certain percentage of them go on to study science in college, and a certain percentage of those become engineers. But if science were required, the number of students studying science would be doubled. At least some of these added students would continue in science, and at least some of them would become engineers. We can assume, then, that adding a science requirement would result in a net gain of engineers.

This argument does not depend on analogy or examples, although such arguments could be offered along with it. This argument is self-contained. It depends on a series of reasonable inferences. An analogous argument would be that the institution of a requirement in the study of fine arts produced a higher number of professional musicians. An argument from example would show that in five countries with science requirements, there are more engineers per capita in the population than in countries without requirements.

Problems with cause-and-effect arguments: As we know from the study of science, one of the challenges in establishing a true sequence of cause and effect is to eliminate extraneous factors. The laboratory is a controlled environment that allows the scientist to isolate and test probable causes for a given effect. The laboratory of the world, of course, cannot be controlled in the same way. The corollary is that there may be many factors contributing to an effect—and those factors may have escaped a chain of logic by which we arrived at a probable cause.

Let's return to our earlier example about the shortage of engineers. Our chain of logic did not consider any economic factors in outlining a cause for the shortage. An economic study might reveal, however, that the decline in the number of students choosing engineering correlates with a rise in the number of students going into banking. A further analysis might show that twenty years ago, engineering was one of the best-paid jobs available to college graduates, but that in today's market, bankers are paid significantly more than engineers are. Our original chain of logic still seems reasonable, but an economic analysis shows that it is far from complete.

In short, the cause-and-effect argument is based on induction. Like any inductive argument, it is incomplete. In debate, the cause-and-effect argument can work well, but it is always vulnerable to an opponent who can offer a different analysis, and a chain of reasoning that leads back to a different cause for the effect under consideration.

Arguments from signs: The argument from signs is similar to the cause-and-effect argument in that it is self-contained, but the logic involved is less rigorous. It, too, is an inductive argument, and is based on phenomena—or signs—that lie outside a causal chain. Let's say that an elected official, with a modest salary, maintains an elaborate home, and two vacation houses. What's more, he is known to entertain lavishly, and to take expensive trips abroad. Based on those signs, we may conclude that he is corrupt, and is either stealing money from the government, or taking bribes. There is no direct evidence—that is, no causal link between a bribe and a vacation—but the signs lead us to a conclusion. Lying behind that conclusion, either explicitly or implicitly, may be an argument from example. We know that in other instances, elected officials with expensive lifestyles have been convicted of corruption.

The argument from signs also uses evidence that is linked statistically, rather than causally. Some studies show, for example, that when unemployment rises, there is a corresponding increase in crime and drug use. The debater citing this statistic doesn't necessarily show why unemployment leads to drug use, but can cite the statistical correlation to argue that if a government proposal is likely to increase unemployment, it will also increase crime and drug use.

Weaknesses of arguments from signs: The argument from signs has the weakness of other inductive arguments. We may conclude that the elected official is corrupt because of the observable signs—but there may be an entirely different explanation for those signs. The official may have income from investments; his spouse may have inherited wealth; his vacation homes may actually belong to friends, and so on. Statistical correlations, in turn, are vulnerable in that they are not reliably predictive; because there is no causal link, there is no reason to believe that something that was statistically true in the past will necessarily be true in the future.

In the preceding pages, we discussed some of the weakness and vulnerabilities in various kinds of argumentative strategies. We also discussed the ways to refute deductive and inductive arguments. Throughout this discussion, however, we have presumed that the arguments being made were fundamentally sound. In the section that follows, we will outline some errors and fallacies that often find their way into unsound arguments.

The hasty generalization: The hasty generalization is basically an argument from examples that has gone awry. A good argument from examples includes a large number of examples. A hasty generalization, however, is based on one or two examples. The Weimar Republic was a weak and corrupt democracy. It does not follow, however, that all democracies are weak and corrupt.

> THE HASTY
> GENERALIZATION
> IS AN
> ARGUMENT
> FROM
> EXAMPLE
> THAT HAS
> GONE AWRY

Under this heading, we can also include the fallacy of using the exception to prove the rule. This also depends on making a general rule from one example. Sometimes in competitive debate, the contestants veer towards extreme cases to try to decide the issue. In one sample resolution in this book, the issue is the use of official language in state schools. A debater who tends to extremes might argue that he can prove the merit of using non-official languages if he can cite even one example that shows that non-official languages are justified. The one example, however, turns out to be a government-run school for deaf-mutes, who are taught primarily in sign language. Sign language is not the official language of the state, and this shows that the state should use non-official languages. The problem is that the example would be an exception to virtually any rule that could be constructed. In other words, the debater has tried to avoid the common meaning of the resolution by focusing on an extreme case.

Post hoc, ergo propter hoc: These Latin words mean, literally, after this, therefore because of this. This is a fallacy that doesn't recognize the difference between after and because. Just because one event comes after another event, it does not mean that the first event was the cause of the second event. It is true that Communism collapsed in Eastern Europe shortly after the uprising in Tianenman Square, but it does not mean that they were related causally. Specifically it does not mean that events in China caused the collapse of communism in Eastern Europe. Along the same lines, it is a fallacy to mistake coincidence for causality. In his discussion of historical causes in *War and Peace,* Tolstoy notes that he can hear church bells every time the hands on his watch indicate the hour—but that doesn't mean that his watch makes the bells ring.

Ad hominem argument: Although the Latin words mean "argument directed at the man," the phrase does not necessarily mean a personal attack on the speaker's opponent. It is not, in essence, an attack on a person, but is, rather, an attempt to discredit an argument by focusing on the character or qualifications of someone who supports it. For example, the issue involved in the resolution may be the state's responsibility to provide universal health care to its citizens. Using the **ad hominem** argument, the debater notes that Adolf Hitler believed in universal health care. The logic is that if a bad person believed in the idea, it must be a bad idea. (Characters like Hitler do not need to be hauled into the argument.) Often enough, it is the character of an opposing politician that is linked with the argument. Because it does not address the ideas themselves, an **ad hominem** argument is not valid form refutation.

Reliance on authority: Although many good debaters will call on the testimony of authorities and experts in order to make their cases persuasive, such testimony is never logically conclusive. It hardly needs to be said that for any controversy imaginable, experts can be cited on either side. It is also worth noting that even laws and constitutions are not the ultimate standard in any competitive debate. History gives us innumerable examples of laws that were immoral and unjust; even enlightened constitutions have been wrong, and have been changed. The United States Constitution was almost a century old before it was amended to give civil rights to black Americans; it was almost 150 years old before it was amended to give voting rights to women. It is illogical to assume that any constitution or body of laws is complete, perfect, and not susceptible to improvement.

Along the same lines, it is not logically powerful to argue that an argument is good because it has been believed for a long time, or by many people. There was once a famous ad campaign for a French cigarette that proclaimed: "Smoke this brand. Forty million Frenchmen can't be wrong." Medical evidence suggests that they were quite wrong, actually.

The non sequitur: In the cast of his play *Rhinoceros*, Eugene Ionesco includes a bumbling logician, who offers this syllogism:

It is clear to the audience that the Logician's conclusion is nonsense; there are many things in the world that are mortal besides cats, so there is no reason to believe that Socrates is a cat, simply because he is mortal. In other words, the syllogism looks logical, and may sound logical, but an examination of the premises shows that there is no causal link. (If, of course, the first premise said that only cats are mortal, the conclusion would be logical—even though it still wouldn't be true.) This error is called a non sequitur, from the Latin phrase meaning, "it does not follow."

The slippery slope: The slippery slope is a logical fallacy that presumes that a chain of events will result because of one single action. If the resolution involves censorship of school newspapers, a debater may invoke the slippery slope to suggest that any restriction in free speech will lead to a restriction of other rights; one step down the slope will lead to another. As a matter of fact, most democratic societies place some limitations on free speech—for instance, by libel laws, or laws forbidding incitement to riot. Such restrictions, however, are not followed by grosser restrictions of civil liberties. The slippery slope is essentially a scare tactic, not a logical argument.

Begging the question: Begging the question is a kind of circular reasoning. It is an argument that acts as if a question that must be asked has already been answered. Say, for example, that someone says, "I want to do this because it is important to me." It looks like a reason is being given, but the only reason offered is a restatement of the initial clause: by definition, we consider something important if we want to do it. Another instance would be to say, "I believe we should do this because it is the right thing to do." Such a statement has little meaning, since the debater hasn't said what he means by the right thing. Allied with this error is the tautology, which offers complete circularity: "I believe that my position is more just because it does a better job of promoting justice."

SUMMARY As we noted above, our aim in offering this description is not to encumber educational debate with logical terms and formalities. We hope, instead, that debaters who are familiar with these terms will become more adept at recognizing the weaknesses in their own arguments, and will improve their cases as a result. And, in the context of competition, students who understand logical fallacies will find it much easier to refute the claims of their opponents.

Chapter 7.
The Affirmative Constructive

In previous chapters, we discussed the function of the affirmative constructive. In essence, it is a speech that makes the affirmative case in full. It presents all the reasons for accepting the affirmative case. In this chapter, we will focus on the form of affirmative constructive. It must be clear and well organized. It must explain what the team wishes to argue and how they intend to argue it. We will also note here that the appendix of this book contains the transcript of an actual debate. The transcript is accompanied by a commentary that indicates the strengths and weaknesses shown by the debaters.

BURDEN OF PROOF Before discussing the affirmative constructive in detail, we should note that in the Karl Popper format there is an equal burden of proof. The existence of a burden of proof means, in essence, that greater weight is given to one side in an argument, as a matter of form. In U.S. criminal court, for example, the prosecution has the burden of proof. A defendant is granted the presumption of innocence. A jury must presume that the defendant is innocent, unless it is clearly proven otherwise by the prosecution. The defense attorney does not have a positive responsibility to prove that his client is a good person. His job, simply, is to refute the charges made by the prosecution, to show that his client is not guilty as charged. If any reasonable doubt about guilt remains after both cases have been presented, the defendant must be found not guilty.

Now, there are debate formats—other than the Karl Popper format—that establish similar burdens for the affirmative side. The judge is instructed to presume that the resolution should be negated, unless the affirmative side can prove clearly otherwise. In other words, the affirmative team carries the burden of proof. This inequality is not as arbitrary as it might seem, however, because resolutions are constructed differently in such a format. That is, the resolutions are not even-handed, as they are in the Karl Popper format, but depend upon the conflict between change (the affirmative team) and the **status quo** (the negative team). A typical resolution might be, "Resolved: Animal cloning should be banned by international agreement." It is implicit in the resolution that animal cloning is not currently banned. Banning represents a change. In other words, the negative team has to defend the status quo. The affirmative team must argue for a change in law and practice. In this format, the status quo is given preference, in the same way that a defendant is presumed innocent in a criminal court. In debate formats that place a burden of proof on the affirmative, the negative team has a similarly limited job. They do not have to prove that the status quo is a great thing. They simply must refute the affirmative team's reasons for making changes.

> IN THE KARL POPPER DEBATE FORMAT THERE IS AN EQUAL BURDEN OF PROOF

As we have indicated, the Karl Popper format is different. And the reason can be traced, in part, back to the nature of resolutions in the Popper format. In Chapter One, we suggested a possible resolution, inspired by the case of General Pinochet: "Resolved: The protection of human rights justifies direct foreign intervention into the domestic affairs of a sovereign nation." Obviously, there is no status quo in this conflict, in the way that there is with the animal cloning resolution above. There is no reason to presume that the negative side is preferable to the affirmative side, and it would not be fair to use such a resolution in a debate format that places the burden of proof on one side.

It is true that sometimes, in the Popper format, the resolution may entail the opposition of change and the status quo. Our model resolution about the legalization of marijuana does just that. But even in these cases, the philosophical stance of the Popper format is that there is no reason why the status quo should be favored. As we have tried to emphasize throughout this book, the ideal resolution, in the Popper format, is one where there is something to be said for both sides. With the burden of proof, the two sides are by definition, unequal. The Popper format rejects that inequality.

What does this mean, in practical terms? It means that the tasks of the two teams in the debate are identical. Both teams must offer cases, with reasons for affirmation and negation, respectively. Both teams have to refute the cases of their opponents. Both teams have to defend themselves against these refutations. Again, in a format that assigns a burden of proof, the tasks are different. The negative team does not have to offer a series of absolute reasons in order to negate the resolution. Instead, they need simply refute the case offered by the affirmative. In the Karl Popper format, simple refutation of the opponent is not enough, for either side. The winning team has to offer a case that is compelling on its own terms.

We will admit that effective refutation sometimes wins by default. A debate can be like a naval battle. It doesn't matter how bad one navy is, or how many ships or sailors it loses, as long as it sinks all the boats on the other side. It wins because the other side lost — and somebody has to win. But Popper debate aspires to a higher level of excellence. Instead of a naval battle, think of a presidential election. What would it mean if a candidate for office confined himself to discrediting his opponent? Surely, voters deserve positive reasons for electing someone. In the clash of values that characterizes Popper debate, judges want to hear positive reasons for affirming the resolution or for negating it. The affirmative debater should be able to say more than, "You should vote for us because negative is wrong." The affirmative debater should be able to say, "You should vote for us because we are right."

THE FORM OF THE CONSTRUCTIVE

As we noted in Chapter Five, many debaters prefer to speak less formally from notes, instead of reading the constructive speech directly from a manuscript, although reading is completely acceptable in the Karl Popper format. But, as we have noted, even if debaters choose not to read the constructive, it should nevertheless be written out in full. This will improve the clarity of the speech, and will foster general understanding by the affirmative team. All three debaters on the team must argue consistently with each other. Each member of the team is responsible for supporting the arguments laid out in the constructive. Therefore, it makes sense for all three members to work together in writing it.

In putting together a case, it is best not to try to do too much. The time given to the constructive is strictly limited to six minutes. If a debater tries to cram ten arguments into that space, those arguments will not be clearly stated or easily understood. As the saying goes, not all arguments are created equal. It is far better to leave the weaker arguments out of the picture, and to focus instead on the best reasons for supporting the resolution. It is better to explain good reasons fully and clearly, instead of sketching weaker reasons in haste.

The Popper format does not precisely dictate the form of the speech. In this chapter, we will offer a model that can be varied or altered as appropriate. The constructive should begin with an introduction that includes a formal statement of the resolution for the debate. It should also define any words in the resolution that are unclear or uncommon. As discussed in Chapter Three, the course of the debate can often be shaped by the way that key terms are defined, and affirmative should establish its definitions at the outset. Next, the constructive should articulate the criterion for judging the debate. The affirmative side should say what value is being upheld by supporting the resolution. As noted, debaters should not cite values that are vague or unclear. It is essential to say, even if only briefly, what is meant by words like justice or democracy, given the context of the resolution. At this point, the debater is offering a standard for judging the debate. He is telling the judge what he intends to prove, and how he intends to prove it. After that, the argument itself can begin. Most of the constructive is devoted to the reasons why the affirmative should be supported; these reasons are sometimes called contentions.

INTRODUCTION

This introductory paragraph should include a statement of the resolution; it should create a context for the resolution, and should suggest to the listener why it is important. This can be accomplished in only a few sentences, but it is an important way to establish the themes of the case. Some debaters like to open with a quote. Others like to use an anecdote. In any case, the introduction should be brief. Most of the time allotted to the constructive should be given to the arguments. It is also customary, in team debate, for the first speaker to introduce himself or herself, and the other members of the team.

DEFINITION OF TERMS

In Chapter Three, we discussed the topic of definitions with reference to the soft drug resolution. As we noted, this resolution is simple and really requires only a few definitions. The affirmative team must make clear what is meant by soft drugs, and what is meant by legalization. These terms do not lend themselves to multiple definitions. With some resolutions, however, the choice of definitions can change the meaning of the resolution entirely. Remember, for example, the other resolution we considered in Chapter Three, about the state's responsibility to provide education only in its official language. In that case, there were a number of possible definitions of the term, each reasonable.

As discussed in Chapter Three, it is not necessary to define every word in the resolution; only the key words need to be addressed. The definitions should be clear and consistent with ordinary language, and should establish grounds for a fair debate; sometimes, it is helpful to quote directly from a source such as a specialized dictionary.

> **DEFINITIONS SHOULD BE NEUTRAL, AND SHOULD NOT GIVE AN UNFAIR ADVANTAGE TO THE AFFIRMATIVE OVER THE NEGATIVE**

Definitions should be neutral, and should not give an unfair advantage to the affirmative over the negative. It should be remembered that the negative side has the prerogative to offer its own definitions of the terms when it presents the negative constructive. If negative does not exercise this prerogative, then the affirmative definitions will stand, and will be used throughout the debate. If negative offers alternative definitions, it must say why those definitions are better than those offered by the affirmative. In effect, the debate then centers on definitions, rather than on values and issues. In other words, it's not a great debate. As a test of fairness, affirmative debaters should ask themselves if they would accept the definitions themselves, if they were arguing on the negative side.

INTRODUCTION OF THE CRITERION

In Chapter Four, we discussed the importance of the criterion at some length. To reiterate: the criterion is really the linchpin of the case, the thing that holds it together. The criterion is the primary value or principle that the team wants to uphold. All of the arguments offered in the case must relate back to the criterion. It is also the standard by which the debate will be judged. As we remarked earlier, the affirmative team is not required to articulate the line of reasoning that led them to choose their criterion— although they may later be challenged by negative proposing another value.

> **ALL OF THE ARGUMENTS OFFERED IN THE CASE MUST RELATE BACK TO THE CRITERION**
>
> **IT IS THE STANDARD BY WHICH THE DEBATE WILL BE JUDGED**

In our model debate about soft drugs, the resolution is open-ended. In other words, there is nothing in the wording of the resolution that suggests or implies a criterion. As a result, debaters have more latitude in defining criteria. It is, therefore, essential to establish clearly articulated criteria. Without such criteria, then there is no basis for judging the debate. In some resolutions, however, the criterion is built-in. Take, for example: "Resolved: Capital punishment is not justified." There, the criterion is justice. The debate will center on how justice is defined, and how it is measured. We should emphasize, however, that built-in criteria do not eliminate the debaters' responsibility to articulate a criterion in the constructive speech: even if the resolution implies that the criterion is justice, the debaters still must say what justice means. As we noted in Chapter Four, justice may mean punishing those who break the law, or it may mean giving each person his due; or it may mean fulfilling one's natural obligations.

We should also note that debaters, in articulating their criteria, should have a clear sense of how these criteria can be measured. If the criterion is, say, justice, how can the affirmative team show that affirming the resolution produces more justice than negating it produces? Is there more justice if more people are convicted of crimes? Or if more people are guaranteed their rights? Or if income and wealth are distributed more evenly throughout the population? Again, those standards of measurement grow out of a precise understanding and articulation of the criterion. And, what is more, they offer a clear agenda for the case and for the debate. The resolution may be, for example, that "a progressive income tax [where wealthier people pay a higher tax rate] is justified." If the affirmative team says that their understanding of justice is the equal distribution of goods throughout society, and that affirming the resolution will maximize that value, it is clear what they intend to prove and how they expect to be measured.

ARGUMENTS As we have noted many times, all of the arguments, or contentions, offered must relate to the central value or principle that has been articulated as the criterion. Sometimes, the case can be constructed syllogistically. Let's use our sample resolution about the state offering education only in its official language to illustrate this. Say that the affirmative team establishes that its criterion is national unity. Its first argument is that the state can use education to create a sense of national identity and unity. Its second argument is that a person's language is something that connects that person with a larger community of people who speak the same language. Finally, its third argument is that linguistic communities tend to create their own socioeconomic communities. The conclusion, which ties the arguments together, is that if the state teaches something other than the official language, it is promoting the creation of autonomous communities. It is using education to produce national disunity, instead of national unity. We described this approach as syllogistic because the individual arguments are not compelling if taken individually and in isolation; a listener might agree with the third argument, that linguistic communities tend to create their own socioeconomic communities, but that in itself would not lead him to agree with the resolution. The argument is persuasive only when all the pieces are put together. If the listener agrees with the first contention, and the second contention, and the third contention, then the conclusion seems reasonable. The same kind of interdependence would be evident if we used Toulmin's model to describe this case.

> **DEBATERS SHOULD HAVE A CLEAR SENSE OF HOW THEIR CRITERIA CAN BE MEASURED**

With other resolutions, other strategies will be appropriate. Say, for example, that affirmative is arguing in favor of a resolution that calls for a state-sponsored arts program because it will benefit the community. One contention might focus on social benefits. The second might focus on economic benefits. The third might focus on the artistic benefits, and so on. The contentions would relate to the central value premise, but would not be related to each other syllogistically. Such an approach is perfectly valid, because, like the syllogism. It is directed at persuading the listener that the resolution is true.

As a matter of form, it is customary to number the arguments, as in the example above. Some speakers like to restate them, in capsule form, as part of the conclusion. For one thing, these signposts help the judge to follow the argument, and to understand the case as it is made. The signposts will help the negative team to understand the case as well. (They, in turn, will offer their own signposts.) In the end, the debate will be clearer for everyone, with these points of reference provided. The negative can say, "I would like to respond to her second contention," rather than, "I would like to respond to what she said about language." It is also customary to conclude the affirmative constructive by inviting cross-examination. The affirmative speaker indicates that the constructive is over, and that she is ready for the next section of the debate.

Chapter 8.
Cross-Examination

In Karl Popper Debate, there are four separate sections of cross-examination: two conducted by members of the affirmative team, and two conducted by members of the negative team. We will begin this chapter with some general remarks about the nature and function of cross-examination, before commenting on the exchanges in the model debate included in the appendix.

THE PURPOSES OF CROSS-EXAMINATION

> THE CROSS-EXAMINATION IS USED FOR PURPOSES OF CLARIFICATION, FINDING WEAKNESSES IN THE OPPONENTS' ARGUMENTS AND GAINING GENERAL CONCESSIONS

In competitive debate, cross-examination performs three distinct functions. First, it is designed to clarify the position that has been taken by the opposing side. If a definition or an argument has been vague, cross-examination gives debaters the chance to demand precision and clarity. Unless the debaters have a clear understanding of what their opponents are saying, they will not be able to refute their arguments. Second, the debater leading the cross-examination can use his questions to probe weaknesses in his opponent's argument. Specifically, he can try to highlight contradictions, and to suggest implications in his opponent's case. Finally, the debater can use the questions to gain general concessions that will support his own case (this tactic was described briefly in Chapter Five). Cross-examination is a set-up for what follows in the debate. The points made in cross-examination should be incorporated into the speeches that follow. As we noted earlier, this calls for teamwork. The person who does the following up is not the person who asked the questions. To use a sports metaphor, the questioner's job is to move the ball towards the goal. The speaker's job is to score.

The following remarks pertain to all four sections of cross-examination. Whether conducted by the affirmative team or the negative team, the nature of the activity does not change.

GROUND RULES

In the cross-examination sections of the debate, the two students involved in the exchange must stand next to each other in the front of the room. They should not, however, face each other directly, either when asking or answering questions. They should, rather, face the audience and the judges. It is natural for the debaters to glance at each other from time to time, but they should keep their main focus on the audience, and should try to maintain eye contact with the judges. Before the cross-examination begins, the questioner will usually use preparation time to consult with teammates and to prepare questions. Once the questioning begins, however, consultation is not allowed. Both the questioner and the respondent must work independently. Cross-examination is meant to consist of an exchange of questions and answers. In other words, it is not a time for either debater to make speeches, or to launch direct attacks on an opponent's position. It is expected that both debaters will be courteous, polite and respectful in word and in manner. Of course, the exchange of question and answer is confined to the debaters; judges and audience members listen and take notes, but they do not participate.

STRATEGY AND TACTICS

In the following discussion, we will talk a bit about tactics, and we would like to clarify the meaning of the word before going on. We are borrowing the words strategy and tactics from military history. The root meaning of strategy is "directing an army." In war, strategy refers to a master plan, to the overall goals of a military campaign. Tactics refers to the methods used to execute that plan. So, a general may have a strategic goal to capture an enemy city on the other side of a river. The tactical question is whether the army should ford the river upstream and attack the town from the land, or whether it should attack it directly by crossing a bridge. In debate, it may be a strategic goal to establish that soft drugs should be legalized; one tactic is to argue by example, another is to argue by analogy, and so on. In cross-examination, debaters use different tactics to achieve their strategic goals.

The questioner should remember that this is not a time to make a speech, but a time to ask questions. Questions can be leading, which is to say they may be aimed at eliciting a specific response. They should never be belligerent or insulting. Generally, the questions should be aimed at eliciting statements, rather than simple yes or no answers. Indeed, it is an unfair tactic to demand such one-word answers, which preclude the nuance and complexity that belong in educational debate. The person answering the question should be given the chance to state a position clearly and honestly. Debaters should not try to imitate the famous lawyerly question, "Is it true that you stopped beating your wife? I want a 'yes' or a 'no' answer!" This is unfair because whatever answer the respondent gives, it is implicit that he did beat his wife at one time.

> QUESTIONS CAN
> BE LEADING,
> HOWEVER, THEY
> SHOULD NEVER
> BE BELLIGERENT
> OR INSULTING

The questioner controls the use of time in this section. The debater asking questions should give his opponent sufficient time to offer a complete response, but may interrupt (politely) if it seems that his opponent is going on too long, or not answering the question directly enough. An interruption is polite if it is made in a respectful tone of voice, and is prefaced with excuse me or the equivalent. If the opponent asks a question herself (instead of giving a response), the questioner should remind her that her team has its own time to ask questions, which will come later, in another section of the debate.

Many lawyers are fond of saying that they don't ask a question in the courtroom unless they already know the answer. That is probably an exaggeration, and it cannot really be achieved in cross-examination; and yet, it is a good principle to keep in mind. The questioner should have a sense of what he wants the respondent to say. He may be disappointed, and get answers he didn't expect, but at least his questions will have specific goals. With these goals in mind, it is easier to phrase questions appropriately. (One technique for leading the respondent is to include options as part of the question being asked—e.g., "You spoke in your constructive speech about your right to speak your own language. Do you regard this as a right, guaranteed by the state? Or is it a natural right?") The goals, of course, are generated in part by the flow—as the affirmative constructive is delivered, members of the negative team should be flagging key points, and generating questions that will focus on them.

As a tactic, many debaters begin by trying to establish grounds of agreement. They ask questions that have only one reasonable answer. After establishing agreement, they move into more controversial areas, where disagreement is seen clearly.

The questioner should remain flexible. During prep time, it makes sense to plan two or three lines of inquiry, but it is a tactical mistake to create a list of questions that is followed in rigid sequence. It is better to listen to what the respondent says, and to ask follow-up questions that will clarify the issue. Remember, of course, that the respondent's tactic is to surrender as a little as possible. The respondent will be wary of making statements that can be used against her, and initial responses will often be noncommittal. Sometimes, the debater answering questions will try to "stonewall"—that is, to avoid answering a question directly, no matter how many times it asked. In such a case, the questioner does best to acknowledge the obfuscation, and move on. He can say, for example, "I can see that I'm not going to get an answer to this question, so let me ask something else." As we will note below, stonewalling is not a smart tactic for the respondent to pursue. It is easy for the questioner's team to exploit this silence in later speeches. (The next speaker may say, for example, "It is clear that our opponents did not want to answer this question, and it's easy to see why: It shows a fundamental weakness in their case."

> IT IS BETTER
> TO USE FEWER
> QUESTIONS
> AIMED AT SPECIFIC
> GOALS DURING
> THE CROSS-
> EXAMINATION

Cross-examination will not be more successful simply if more questions get asked; it is better to use fewer questions aimed at a specific goal. It is also better to maintain focus, and to follow a line of inquiry, rather than asking random questions that wander over the opponent's case. Questions that are poorly phrased will rarely yield useful answers. Valuable time is wasted if the question has to be rephrased because it was unclear, but debaters should not be afraid to rephrase questions if they are not understood by opponents. It is also a mistake to ask long and complicated questions. It is better to be pithy and direct. Occasionally, it is a good tactic to pursue an analogical lino of quootion. Eay, for oxample, that the rcsolution is about the legalization of marijuana. In cross-examination, the debater may choose to build a line of questioning around alcohol, without making the connection to the resolution explicit. In a later speech, the debater then makes the point of the analogy clear. As a tactic, analogical questions can sometimes elicit admissions from the opponent; because the resolution is not being addressed directly, the opponent may be more willing to give direct and unguarded answers. Analogies that are strained or farfetched, however, are not often successful. The same can be said about hypothetical questions. It may work to ask, "If you knew that you were going to spend the rest of your life in Sweden, would you make plans to learns Swedish?" Debaters should resist the temptation, however, to ask questions that begin, "Let's say we lived on another planet, and on this planet there are two hair colors, and two languages."

QUESTIONERS CAN SIT DOWN BEFORE THE ALLOTTED THREE MINUTES HAVE BEEN CONSUMED

Finally, questioners should not be afraid to make a graceful exit before the allotted three minutes have been consumed. Sometimes, of course, the three minutes will not seem long enough, and time will run out in mid-question. (A word of advice: questioners should not leave the most important question until last.) But if the questioner has made his points, and asked what he wanted to ask before time runs out, it is wise to close the questioning and sit down. It is a mistake to continue with weak or unprepared questions; they may lead to tactical losses, and they will leave the audience with a negative impression of the section as a whole.

ADVICE FOR THE RESPONDENT

Respondents in cross-examination need to be careful and cautious, but that does not mean they should be cowardly. They should be careful because the questioners are attempting to get them to say things that will weaken their cases. The respondent needs to listen to the questions carefully, and to be alert to subtle implications that may be contained in them. The respondent should also think carefully before answering. Answers must be direct and precise. Questions should be answered fully, but respondents should not answer more than was asked. And yet, respondents should not be afraid to take strong stands. After all, they have entered the debate to argue a specific position, and they should not back away from that position when it is challenged. It is a good tactic to qualify answers in a way that reinforces that position, by reasserting an argument. This tactic is especially good when the questioner demands a "yes" or "no" answer; even if the questioner will interrupt to cut off a more nuanced answer, it is wise to try to establish a context for that yes or no response.

It is also fair for respondents to qualify leading questions. The questioner may ask a question with two alternatives. The respondent can certainly suggest a third answer—as long as it does not seem that she is avoiding the question. Along the same lines, it is possible for the respondent to reject analogies or hypothetical statements by casting doubt on the relevance of the comparison or rejecting the relevance of the hypothesis, as the case may be.

THROUGHOUT THE CROSS-EXAMINATION THE RESPONDENT SHOULD STRIVE TO GIVE HONEST, POLITE, AND RESPECTFUL ANSWERS

It is perfectly acceptable to ask for clarification of questions that are unclear or poorly phrased. It is not a wise tactic, however, to plead misunderstanding simply as a way to avoid answering the question. The question will be rephrased and asked again, and it must be answered. Delaying an answer doesn't improve it. When a respondent refuses to answer a question, the listener will assume, generally, that the respondent thinks his own position is weak, and would be made weaker by answering. It is also unwise for the respondent to disagree simply for the sake of disagreeing. If, for example, the questioner were to say, "I think we can agree that it is dark at night," the respondent is unwise to answer, "Well, I'm not sure about that—it all depends on what you mean by the word 'dark.'" Debate is supposed to involve discussion, and engagement on issues—not obfuscation and avoidance.

Finally, there is nothing wrong with admitting ignorance when appropriate. If the questioner asks the respondent if he knows how many languages are spoken in India, and he doesn't know, there is no point in trying to fake it. Throughout the cross-examination, respondents should strive to give honest answers. And their answers should also be polite and respectful. Questions can be hostile, but so can answers. It is incumbent upon questioners to avoid the former, and it is incumbent upon respondents to avoid the latter.

Chapter 9.
The Negative Constructive and Refutation

As indicated in Chapter Four, this section of the debate has a dual function. First, the negative team must lay out its case against the resolution in a constructive speech. Second, the negative team must begin its attack against the affirmative case. The constructive part of this speech is not fundamentally different from the affirmative constructive. It, too, must lay out the entire negative argument against the resolution. Because of time constraints, it will be shorter, to allow time for refutation. But in composing the negative constructive, debaters should follow the guidelines offered for the affirmative constructive outlined in Chapter Seven. The following discussion will focus on the refutation part of this speech.

STRATEGIC CONCERNS

For the negative team, this is a critical moment in the debate. They must decide on the most efficient and effective plan of attack on the affirmative position. They cannot attack everything. A global attack would be too unfocused, and individual points would get scanty attention. At the same time, they cannot limit their attack to only one target. It is rare that a case will be refuted because of only one flaw. What is more, negative has to remember that it, too, will be attacked, and its case will be weakened at some points. The winning side in a debate does not often emerge completely unscathed. The winner, rather, has the case that remains the most persuasive on balance, even if it has been weakened at some points. It is helpful here to think of the different levels of the affirmative case. The affirmative team has offered definitions. They have offered a criterion. They have offered arguments. Negative can attack at any level.

CONFLICT ABOUT DEFINITIONS

We indicated, in our discussion of definitions, that some resolutions allow for considerable latitude in the way that they are defined. In its constructive speech, the affirmative team has defined the terms of the resolution in the way that suits them. Before the negative team presents their own case in the negative constructive speech, they must decide whether or not to accept those definitions. According to the rules of Popper debate, the definitions of the affirmative will stand as accepted unless they are challenged by the negative side. It is rare, of course, for the affirmative team to define the terms in exactly the same way that the negative team would. The negative team must decide if the differences are worth fighting about. In our model debate, the affirmative team has defined soft drugs as the cannabis derivatives, marijuana and hashish. What if negative had written its case with the understanding that soft drugs also include amphetamines, and recreational drugs like Ecstasy? The question they must ask themselves is whether they can still make their case against the resolution with the more limited definition offered by the affirmative. If they can, they should let the definition stand, and concentrate on more substantial differences.

UNDER THE RULES OF KARL POPPER DEBATE, THE AFFIRMATIVE DEFINITIONS WILL STAND AS ACCEPTED UNLESS THEY ARE CHALLENGED BY THE NEGATIVE TEAM

Sometimes, a negative challenge is necessary. If the affirmative definitions are narrow or skewed, if the affirmative team tried to define soft drugs as cough suppressants containing codeine, the negative team would have to mount a challenge. Negative would also have to mount a challenge if its case depended essentially on a different understanding of the resolution. Say, for example, that negative wanted to argue that legalization meant completely unlimited distribution of soft drugs, through an open market, and affirmative had defined legalization to mean distribution only through government agencies.

As we noted when discussing definitions back in Chapter Seven, debates that revolve around definitions usually don't offer the clash of values and ideas that characterize a good debate. This kind of olash occurs in definitional debates only when the term being defined has a significant content—e.g., when the argument is about the definition of the word justified. It is best if definitions are neutral, and acceptable to both sides. If the differences are minor, the negative team does well to leave them be, and to focus its attention on more important matters.

CONFLICT ABOUT CRITERIA

Fundamentally, there are three kinds of conflict possible here. First, the affirmative and negative sides can argue in favor of completely different criteria, which conflict with each other. Second, both sides can argue in favor of the same criterion, nominally, but disagree about the definition and meaning of that value. For example, both sides can say that they are supporting justice, but they can understand that word in different ways. Third, both sides can agree about the criterion, and its meaning, but they can disagree about how to measure that value and how to maximize it. Again, both sides can argue in favor of justice, and agree that it means giving each one his due, but they can disagree about which course of action, the one implied by affirming the resolution, or the one implied by negating it, is more just. In this case, the argument is really about the truth of supporting arguments, a conflict that is discussed more fully in the next section.

> **IF NEGATIVE CHOOSES TO CHALLENGE THE CRITERION THEY MUST ADDRESS IT BEFORE ANSWERING THE AFFIRMATIVE ARGUMENTS**

If negative decides to argue about conflicting criteria, it assumes a dual burden. It is true, as a matter of logic, that if the criterion of the opposing side is thoroughly discredited, then the arguments in support of that criterion have little worth. But negative cannot assume that its refutation of the affirmative criterion will be successful. Accordingly, it must argue from a hypothetical standpoint: "Even if you accept the affirmative criterion (and I do not), their argument is false for the following reasons." The dual burden is this: Negative first must argue against the criterion, and then must argue against the arguments supporting that criterion.

CONFLICT ABOUT ARGUMENTS

The negative team may choose not to give battle over definitions. It may also choose not to give battle over the criterion. It cannot avoid conflicting with the affirmative over arguments, however. Indeed, this is where most conflicts are centered in debate, and a good debate is structured to make those conflicts clear and apparent. The affirmative side should number its arguments as they are presented; negative should respond to them with precision. The negative speaker should announce, for example, "Their third argument was that countries with disparate language groups can never be unified. I disagree." Arguments can be refuted in different ways. They may be refuted as logically flawed or factually inaccurate. They may be refuted as extreme or prejudicial. They may be refuted as inconsistent with other arguments, or with statements made during cross-examination.

> **A GOOD DEBATE IS STRUCTURED TO MAKE CONFLICTS CLEAR AND APPARENT**

In Chapter Five, we listed some of the logical errors that may be pointed out in the course of a refutation. If the affirmative team offers analogies, a good refutation will attack the validity of those analogies. If the affirmative case depends heavily on external authorities—that is, what someone else said that might support the resolution—a good refutation will attack the competence, credibility, or impartiality of those authorities, and offer words from other authorities in return. The affirmative case might also be attacked on the grounds of irrelevance, or insignificance. With the last tactic, the refutation says, in so many words, that while a contention may be true, it is not important. In our model debate, for example, the affirmative team argues that the legalization of drugs will increase the tax revenues of the state. The negative team admits that this is true, but argues that it does not constitute a sufficient reason for legalization, because the wrong done by legalization outweighs the benefit of increased tax revenues.

SOME RULES FOR THE NEGATIVE REFUTATION

We have emphasized above the strategic importance of the decision that negative must make. We have indicated that if the definitions offered by affirmative are not challenged, they must stand. The same can be said for the criterion. To some degree, the same can be said about the arguments. The negative team is expected to respond to the affirmative case fully at this point; it is not allowed to introduce completely new objections at a later point in the debate. That is, they cannot say in their next rebuttal, "I now would like to address my opponent's third argument." The same principle, actually, has bound the affirmative team: they were expected to present a full case in the constructive. They cannot say later in the debate, "I have a new criterion," or "I would like to offer a new argument." Of course, there is much of the debate still to come after this point, and the arguing is hardly over. But, as far as the negative side is concerned, the issues have been identified. They may not have made all of their arguments, but they have established what they intend to argue about.

We offer one final thought: The strategic importance of this moment means that good flow is essential for the negative team. They must pay careful attention to the affirmative constructive, and to affirmative answers during cross-examination; they must analyze these statements, and quickly map out the negative response. Again, we will emphasize that the refutation is not presented by the same person who has conducted the cross-examination; it is essential that the negative speaker listen carefully to the cross-examination, and note the weaknesses that have been exposed and the admissions that have been made. A portion of the negative speech may be read, although most debaters, at this point, like to depart from the text to incorporate remarks that will highlight their contrast with the affirmative. Most of the speech is reactive and responsive. If, at this point in the debate, the negative team adopts the wrong strategy, or misses the key issues, they are not likely to win the debate.

> **GOOD FLOW IS ESSENTIAL FOR THE NEGATIVE TEAM**

There is no one way to conduct a refutation. It really depends on what the other side has argued in the first place. Whatever tactics are used, the refutation should move to a strong conclusion. The negative speaker should sum up, in a few words, his sense of the implications of the affirmative argument, and why he stands opposed. The future direction of the debate is now almost entirely clear. With the affirmative refutation of the negative, the final pieces will fall into place.

Chapter 10.
Affirmative Refutation and Rebuttal

THE DIFFERENCE BETWEEN REFUTATION AND REBUTTAL

In Chapter Nine, we discussed the nature of refutation. To refute an argument means to disprove it, by pointing out flaws in logic, support, or consistency. This is an offensive tactic. When a debater refutes an argument, he is on the attack. He is directing his energy at his opponent's position. Rebuttal, on the other hand, is defensive. The debater's own position has been attacked by his opponent. In a rebuttal, he is trying to reestablish the validity of his position.

The functional distinction between refutation and rebuttal is real. In the everyday language of competitive debate, however, we tend not to be obsessed with the precise use of the terms. In practice, "rebuttal" is an umbrella word that is used to describe not only genuine rebuttal, but refutation as well. This causes no great difficulties, however, and actually reflects a reality. As we will see, refutation and rebuttal become intertwined in later stages of debate. In this chapter, we make the distinction between the two terms simply because we want to emphasize the dual nature of the affirmative speech.

THE DUAL NATURE OF THE AFFIRMATIVE SPEECH

Part of the second affirmative speech is refutation. It parallels the first negative speech: at that point, negative had heard the affirmative case, and, in its speech, attempted to refute it. Negative also, at that time, offered its own case. Now, affirmative has the chance to refute that case. Again, thoroughness is an important standard. The affirmative team must offer, even if only in abbreviated form, their objections to the negative case. It is not fair to introduce new objections at a later juncture. The techniques of refutation that can be used by the affirmative team here are the same as those discussed, in the context of the negative refutation, in the last chapter.

But this section of the debate also offers something new. In their first speech, the negative team attacked the affirmative case. Now, the affirmative team has the task of responding to that attack.

STRATEGIES FOR REBUTTAL

A good rebuttal does not consist of simply repeating the original affirmative case. A rebuttal is, in a sense, a refutation of a refutation. The debater must address each of the arguments that her opponent has made against her case. The techniques used in rebuttal are not radically different from those used in refutation. The debater making the rebuttal has to find flaws in logic, presumptions, or evidence in her opponent's refutation. A successful challenge will restore the validity of the original argument. To be more specific: In the constructive speech, the affirmative team has offered an argument; the negative team has attempted to disprove that argument in their refutation. If, in this rebuttal, the debater can show that the refutation was unfair, untrue, or misdirected, then the original argument stands as true. In practice, the opponent will get another chance to refute, and the debater will get another chance to rebut; this is the sequence of the closing rounds of the debate.

This speech is challenging because the speaker has to cover so much ground. The affirmative speaker will always have the double burden of refutation and rebuttal that is outlined above, but the task can be multiplied by various levels of conflict. If negative has decided to attack both the criterion and the arguments of the affirmative case, that means that the affirmative speaker has more to respond to in her rebuttal. It also means that she is more or less forced to attack in a parallel way; her criterion has been attacked so she must attack her opponent's criterion in return. The bottom line is that if conflict in this debate were limited to the level of arguments, the affirmative would have to make fewer points, and would have more time for each.

As a matter of fairness, refutation should take priority here. Affirmative must introduce her objections to the negative case in full at this point in the debate; she cannot offer new points in the penultimate section of the round, although she will be free to reassert her objections in a different way, incorporating material from the ensuing sections. Negative will rebut her refutations; she can criticize that rebuttal, and reassert her refutation. The task of rebuttal is not so strictly limited to this moment. She will have another opportunity to rebut attacks. If time is short, it is acceptable to sketch out a line of defense that can be amplified later.

Again, signposts should offer the listeners clarity. The affirmative speaker must be explicit about what is being addressed. It is especially important for the speaker to distinguish between when she is attacking the arguments of the negative case and when she is rebutting the attacks they have made on the affirmative case.

Finally, the affirmative speaker should try to conclude by making some observations about where the debate seems to be headed. Even though half of the sections of the debate still lie ahead, both sides have already established their basic positions by this point. Each team has laid out its case in full, in the constructive speeches. Each team has had a chance to indicate, in the refutations, where it will attack its opponent. At this juncture, the affirmative speaker is able to summarize where the essential differences are, and to set an agenda for the remainder of the debate.

Chapter 11.
Concluding Arguments

In the preceding chapters, we examined some sections of the debate round in detail. With each section of the debate that we considered, we encountered new modes of debate, such as refutation and rebuttal. In the three speeches remaining for consideration, there are no new modes. The debaters will refute, and rebut, just as they did before. But as the debate moves towards its conclusion, its focus will become narrower. Each debater will try to articulate the central conflicts in the round. In this chapter, we'd like to offer a few words about that process.

PRIOR PRESENTATION OF ISSUES

As we remarked in our last chapter, dealing with the affirmative refutation and rebuttal, all of the major issues in the debate round have emerged by the end of this speech. That is partly the result of the design of the Karl Popper format. As we have said before—and as we will emphasize again, here—both teams are expected to present *complete* cases during their opening speeches. In those speeches, definitions are offered, the criteria are articulated, and the arguments are made. After that point, there are no changes in the definitions allowed. The criteria cannot be changed, nor can arguments be added to the case. The debate, in a sense, becomes an argument about something that has already been said. The refutations focus on what has been said in the cases. The rebuttals focus on what has been said in the refutations.

In the final three speeches, there is still interplay of refutation and rebuttal. But refutation and rebuttal can sometimes start to look like an endless cycle of argument. That is, affirmative argues, and negative refutes, then affirmative rebuts the refutation, and negative repeats the refutation claiming that the rebuttal was not accurate, and then affirmative rebuts the same point again before negative repeats the refutation yet again...and then the final bell rings. In the best debates, however, the final speeches do not keep sending the same balls back and forth over the net.

IDENTIFICATION OF MAJOR CONFLICTS

For one thing, the final speeches should aim at making some discriminations about the disagreements that have emerged. It should be clear, by now, that some points of contention are more significant than others are. Debaters can start to see what the conflict is really about. In the model debate, contained in our appendix, it becomes clear, after a certain point, that the debate really hinges on how harmful soft drugs are. Specifically, one team wants to argue that soft drugs are minimally harmful, and harm only the user. The other team wants to argue that the use of soft drugs has a significant impact on other people. Now, neither team said, at the very beginning when they made their constructive speeches, that this would be the central issue in the debate. Rather, through cross-examination and refutation, it is how the argument happened to develop. It's possible, too, that another central issue might have emerged. The two teams disagreed about whether the state has the right to keep individuals from harming themselves, but this disagreement did not dominate their exchanges.

VOTING ISSUES

What this means, practically, is that the debaters who make the final speeches for each team should not be trying to think of new ways of making old arguments. They should, rather, be trying to reduce the conflict to its simplest form. In some cases, the best debaters are able to frame what are called **voting issues**. Again, we will refer to the model debate in our appendix. Both sides, in this debate about the legalization of soft drugs, have articulated the benefits to society as their criterion. And both sides, somewhat unusually, have agreed that society will benefit from the reduction in drug use. The affirmative team has argued that the legalization of soft drugs will make them less desirable, and usage will drop. The negative team, on its side, has argued that the ban on soft drugs is an effective deterrent, and legalization will increase drug use. What this means, really, is that they are disagreeing about the best way to reduce drug use—and that is a voting issue. Either team can say, "Would you agree that if I can show that my way is better, then I win the debate?" In other words, the debate has been boiled down to a single decisive factor. By the way, you will not find this voting issue articulated in the model debate, as neither side brought it into clear focus.

SUMMATION OF THE ROUND

To some degree, then, the final speeches are self-referential. That is, they comment on the debate. In that function, they can also review what has happened: it is particularly appropriate, in the final speeches, for speakers to draw the judge's attention to how arguments have ended. Here, speakers invoke the principle that silence means consent. In other words, if the opposing team has not refuted an argument, or rebutted a refutation, it is assumed that they agree with the argument (in the first case), or with the refutation (in the second). In the jargon of debate, leaving an argument unanswered is called dropping a argument. The speaker can say, for example, "Our team refuted their second argument, but they really did not rebut our criticism. So we have to assume that by dropping the point, they have conceded it, and accept that our refutation was true." This is sometimes called instructing the judge, and it can be an effective technique, within limits. Judges are supposed to be keeping their own scorecards of what has been refuted, and are aware that debaters sometimes are a bit too eager to claim victory. After all, judges are capable of deciding themselves whether or not a refutation has been effective. We should also note, in this context, that the final judgment in a debate is not based on technical points. It may be true that the negative team did not bother to rebut an affirmative refutation, but that may be because they did not consider it to be important. The negative team may, instead, have focused its energy on showing that the affirmative criterion was vague and inappropriate. And it goes without saying that if the criterion is discredited, the case as a whole has no merit, even if the individual arguments are allowed to be true.

In sum, then, the final speeches are not more of the same. They are not supposed to be a continuation of the original case, and they are not supposed to be a repetition of what has been said already. They call, instead, for powers of analysis. The final speakers should isolate the most important points that have been made in an argument that has lasted better than half an hour. They must be able to say why, in the final analysis, their team has argued more persuasively.

Chapter 12.
Delivery and Style

So far in this book, we have talked a great deal about the content of competitive debate. We have discussed the nature of argumentation, logical strategies, and the like. But we have said little about the way that arguments are delivered; we haven't focused on speaking style. Our concentration on content has been deliberate. The essence of the competition is substance, not style. And yet, style is significant in any public speaking event, and we will turn our attention to it in this chapter.

SOME OBSERVATIONS ABOUT LANGUAGE

Before turning our attention to delivery, we would like to offer a few observations about the language of debate. Since so much of competitive debate is spontaneous and reactive, it is impossible for debaters to polish their prose into fancy rhetoric. In the context of debate, however, simpler is often better. In the discussion of oratorical style that follows we will emphasize the importance of clarity in delivery. Debaters should also aim for clarity of thought, diction, and organization.

> **DEBATERS SHOULD AIM FOR CLARITY OF THOUGHT, DICTION, AND ORGANIZATION**

Clear diction is language that avoids jargon. Debaters must be careful not to speak their own exclusive language. Even the word "criterion" does not mean much to the uninitiated listener. That listener will, however, understand a debater who says, "In this debate, I intend to support justice as my primary value." Debaters also need to be careful to avoid using shorthand and abbreviations. An example of shorthand is when a debater says, "My argument is true because of the social contract"— without further elaboration. An example of abbreviation is when a debater says, "I argued that in my first AR," with AR meaning affirmative rebuttal.

Clear organization is organization that is, to some degree, self-referential. Any good writer follows an outline, but that outline is rarely made explicit. In debate, however, the structure of the debate and its principles of organization should be made clear. We discussed some of this earlier, in describing the sections of the debate round. We noted that it is important to number arguments, for instance. It also promotes clear understanding if the debater announces a plan of intent before beginning, for example, "First, I will offer my own arguments before moving on to my opponent's case. I will offer three contentions in support of this resolution." As the debate develops, it is also important to summarize, and create a clear focus.

ORATORICAL STYLE IN DEBATE

Yet another aspect of debate is oratorical style. Oratory may be understood in purely technical terms. A good orator is someone who uses his voice well, by modulating its pitch and volume. Orators manage the speed at which they talk. They use pauses and silences for dramatic effect. A good orator uses his body as well as his voice. Facial expression, gesture, and movement are all used to communicate with the audience.

> **TRUTH IS POWERFUL ONLY IF IT CAN BE HEARD**

Again, oratorical skill can be considered independently of content. In many speech competitions, for instance, participants are asked to recite speeches that were composed by someone else. They are not judged on the basis of the quality of the speech, or of its ideas. They are judged purely as interpreters, on the basis of the way that they deliver their text.

Obviously, debate in the Karl Popper format is not an exercise in oratorical interpretation. And yet, oratorical skill has its place in the competition. After all, a debater can arrive at a tournament with a brilliantly prepared case, and may dominate every exchange with her opponent in the round, but no one will be convinced if she is inaudible beyond the first row of the audience. Truth is powerful, but only if it can be heard.

Debate is a public event. It is an act of communication with an audience, which includes judges. If it were an essay contest, judges could consider the strength of a competitor's argument in an atmosphere of quiet reflection. Words on a page can be read and reread many times before they are judged. But in competitive debate, the arguments have a fleeting existence. They must persuade the judge even as they are made, and pass from the debater's mouth to the judge's ear. If the debater has oratorical skill, those arguments will be heard and understood better. The substance of the argument is still what is most important, but debaters have to make sure that substance gets delivered to its intended audience.

FINDING A PERSONAL STYLE

We must say, at the outset, that there is no such thing as a perfect oratorical style. That is, there is no one model that debaters should study and try to copy. Style is a reflection of personal strengths, both physical and mental. Some speakers have naturally mellifluous voices; some don't. Some speakers use strong hand gestures in everyday conversation, and carry them over easily to the debate room; other speakers are more passive. Some speakers are witty as a matter of routine; some speakers are earnest and sober. A successful style is one that capitalizes on personal strengths, whatever they are. Generally, debaters will seem silly if they try to adopt someone else's style. Luciano Pavarotti and Elvis Presley are both great singers, but you wouldn't want to see Elvis in *Rigoletto*, and no one would buy a record of Pavarotti singing *Jailhouse Rock.* As simple as it sounds, debaters must be themselves. Listeners will respond better to a style that is honest and authentic, rather than forced and artificial.

SOME GENERAL PRECEPTS

Style is personal, but there are some standards to which all must adhere. Singers have personal styles, but they all have to sing on key.

The first standard in debate is clarity. Debaters must speak clearly, so that they can be clearly understood. That means, for starters, that debaters must enunciate words clearly; they must not mumble, or slur words, or swallow syllables. This does not mean that they have to over-enunciate in an unnatural way, but they should emulate the natural clarity of a television newsreader. In everyday conversation, we sometimes become lazy about enunciation, because our conversational partners will interrupt us to ask, "What did you say?" In debate, however, there are no clarifying interruptions. If the words are not understood as they are spoken, they are lost forever. One of the great enemies of clarity in debate is speed. Some debaters deliberately try to talk fast in order to cram more arguments into their allotted time, and some debaters speak faster than normal because they are nervous. But listeners rarely understand rapid speech. This is particularly true when the content of the speech is abstract or subtle. Debaters are advised, as a rule, to slow down: listeners' understanding of the arguments will increase proportionately.

> DEBATERS MUST SPEAK CLEARLY, SO THAT THEY CAN BE CLEARLY UNDERSTOOD

Finally, we encourage debaters to pause for breath, once in a while. Such pauses help them to relax and collect their thoughts before saying the next word. Listeners are never confused by a short pause. They may be confused, however, if the speaker rushes forward and stumbles over his own words.

The second standard of debate is audibility. Debaters must speak loudly enough to be heard. They must project their voices at a volume higher than what is used in normal conversation. In normal conversation, our listeners may be five feet away, but in a debate round, the judge may be sitting thirty feet away. At that distance, a normal speaking voice may be inaudible. This doesn't mean, however, that debaters have to shout. Too much can be as bad as too little. If the judge is sitting thirty feet away, the debater does not need to use a volume suitable for a football stadium. Listeners would feel that they are being yelled at, and quickly grow weary of the assault. The task for the debaters is to find the appropriate level for the rooms they are in. Experienced debaters will learn to read signals from the audience: listeners

> DEBATERS MUST PROJECT THEIR VOICES AT A VOLUME HIGHER THAN WHAT IS USED IN NORMAL CONVERSATION

will usually convey that they are unable to hear, either through their facial expressions, or by leaning forward bodily.

The third standard concerns emphasis and variety of expression. It is helpful to approach this standard by thinking of logical structure. In any speech, there are statements of primary importance, and statements of secondary importance. If the speech is well crafted, those distinctions will be explicitly articulated. But they should also be indicated by the speaker's delivery. If the entire speech is delivered without variety, big points and little points become indistinguishable. If the whole speech is delivered in a quiet monotone, it is like looking at a broad plain, with no distinguishing characteristics; if the whole speech is delivered with unvarying passionate intensity, it is like looking at a plateau: the land is higher, but it's still not very interesting. A good speech, to pursue this metaphor, has the hills and valleys of a picturesque landscape.

Speakers can use many tools to emphasize their main points. They can slow down; they can speak more loudly, or more softly; they can raise or lower the pitch of their voices. They can pause before a key statement, or after it. They can even repeat important phrases if they choose. Again, there is not one right way to do this: the tools that are used are a part of a speaker's personal style. But the standard applies to everyone. Every debater must use expressive tools to emphasize the structure of his argument.

The fourth standard concerns the use of gestures and movement. In everyday life, most of us use gestures when we speak. We move our hands, we shake our heads, we change the way we are standing or sitting, all as a way of reinforcing what we are saying with words. But we don't usually think about our gestures as we are making them. There is not a little part of our conscious mind that says: "Now I will clench my right hand because I am angry." In other words, our ordinary gestures happen naturally.

In debate, however, it often happens that something short-circuits the natural impulse to gesture. Debaters start thinking about gestures—and they start worrying about what to do with their hands. (Sometimes, they worry about each hand individually, thinking, *I am making a gesture with my right hand, but what should I be doing with my left hand? I can't just let it hang there at the end of my arm, can I?*) When debaters start thinking about gestures, they usually become artificial, and the audience picks that up. If the speaker seems uncomfortable, and the gestures seem artificial, the listeners start to feel uncomfortable watching—and they start to suspect the sincerity of the speaker. Listeners are also distracted by gestures that are repeated endlessly, like tics; constant finger pointing, for example, becomes its own center of attraction. The audience stops listening to the speech, and starts watching the finger. The point of using gestures is to reinforce, or emphasize, what is being said. Unvarying gestures provide no emphasis. And certain gestures provide no emphasis at all. Speakers should avoid playing with their hair, pulling on their lapels, and putting their hands in their pockets, and so on. Neither is it a good idea to make gestures with props—for example, a pen, or a flow chart. The flow chart can, in fact, be a handicap for many debaters. It should be positioned in front of the speaker for easy reference, if necessary, but it should not be clutched and waved in the air; neither should the speaker deliver his speech while bent double over a desk, with his nose buried in his notes.

It is impossible to make the debater's self-consciousness go away completely. Unlike a speaker in an ordinary conversation, the debater is keenly aware of being watched. Nevertheless, speakers should do what they can to relax and to let gestures happen naturally. Of course, it's hard *not* to think about something—as in the famously impossible mental exercise: "For the next thirty seconds, do not think about an elephant." But speakers can help themselves by concentrating on something else: if they think more about maintaining eye contact (see below), they won't worry as much about gestures.

Similar observations can be made about movement. A speaker can walk a few paces, or stand still, as a way of emphasizing what she is saying. Movement can even mirror the structure of a speech, if the speaker moves a step or two in one direction while making her first contention, and moves in the other direction for her second contention. But again, movement will be effective only if it is natural, or seems natural. Listeners are unlikely to be persuaded by debaters who seem to be executing a choreographic routine.

When addressing an audience, eye contact is extremely important. In some kinds of performance, it is a convention to pretend that the audience does not exist. In many plays, for example, actors confine their attention to the other actors, and the little world of the stage; the audience is allowed to overhear their conversations. This is not, however, a convention in debate. The listeners in the room are not simply overhearing an argument between the debaters; those debaters are actively trying to persuade the audience to share their respective positions.

In short, debate is not an act of performance; it is an act of communication, even though the audience remains silent throughout the debate. All of the foregoing remarks, actually—about clarity, audibility, emphasis, and gesture—should be understood in that context. The speakers want to be heard, they want to be understood, and they want to be believed. The listeners, for their part, want to feel that the speakers are speaking to them. A debater cannot afford; then, to concentrate his attention on his other teammates, or on the opposing team, or on the ceiling, or on the wall, or on what is outside the window. He needs to focus on his audience; he needs to make eye contact.

Usually, it takes speakers a while to develop this skill. At first, it can make them nervous to look at their listeners, and see how they are reacting. An old trick used by neophyte speakers is to shift their target slightly. Instead of looking directly into a listener's eyes, they focus on the bridge of his nose. It is also difficult, at first, to feel comfortable about shifting focus: the debater cannot spend all of her time looking at one face, but must shift focus, and make eye contact with a number of people in the room. But with time, most debaters develop an instinct for such shifts; ideally, they mirror the rhythms of the speaker's thoughts. A good speaker does not follow an internal stopwatch, with ten seconds of eye contact for one listener, and ten seconds for the next. The shifts will take place, instead, at the end of a sentence, or at the conclusion of an idea. With practice (and relaxation), shifting focus becomes a natural movement, rather than a conscious effort.

Of course, if a room is large, or crowded, it isn't possible for debaters to make eye contact with everyone in the room. But fortunately, listeners are generous in their expectations. A person sitting in a crowd doesn't mind that much if the speaker never focuses on him individually, as long as she seems to be focusing on *somebody*, and not on a point on the floor. Some debaters find it daunting to make sufficient contact in a large room. It can help, therefore, to have friends "planted" in different parts of the audience; they can serve as focal points that help to spread the range of the speaker's contact. Debaters want to make sure, however, to include their judges on their contact lists. Especially in a large room, it is important for debaters to know where their judges are sitting before the round begins.

We have mentioned earlier that some debaters like to read their constructives from written texts, and this is certainly appropriate. Debaters should know their texts very well, however, so that their eyes don't remain glued to the page; they need to look up, and to include the audience regularly. The same principle should guide their use of notes during cross-examination, and rebuttal speeches; they should be able to use the notes quickly, while maintaining their primary focus on the audience. Accordingly, debaters do well to write their notes clearly, and in a large size; they can't afford to spend time staring at a page, trying to decipher a squiggle of handwriting.

The best speakers in debate are individuals who come across as natural, relaxed, and authentic; they are believable because they seem like they are being themselves. It is ironic that it takes a lot of practice to achieve that natural state. But practice helps speakers to lose artificial worries. It is similar to what happens in the theatre: an actor who spends his time on stage worrying if he'll remember his next line, or where he has to stand, is never going to give a convincing performance as a character. After weeks of rehearsal, however, those worries should disappear, and a convincing performance becomes possible. The actor is able to focus his attention properly. With practice, debaters stop worrying about all the mechanics that go into oratory; and they are able to concentrate on their audience, and on their message. When the artificial worries disappear, nature takes over.

Part of the practice, of course, comes from the experience of regular competitions. But debaters can also benefit significantly from intramural rehearsal. Coaches and teammates can play the part of objective observers, and react to the debater's use of oratorical mechanics. This is especially valuable for eliminating bad habits, which are often unconscious; a debater may not realize, sometimes, that his voice has fallen into a singsong pattern, or that his gestures have become repetitive.

Chapter 13.
The Debate Club in the School Community

We began this book with a discussion of the role of debate in a democratic society. Now, as we approach our conclusion, we will discuss the role of educational debate in a school community.

THE BENEFITS OF DEBATE AS AN EDUCATIONAL ACTIVITY

In our opening discussion, we emphasized that competitive debate is directly modeled on debate outside the schoolhouse. In a very real sense, students who participate in debate are preparing themselves for citizenship. They are preparing themselves to participate in the life of the society in which they live. That does not mean that they will necessarily become politicians or civil servants, although they may. It does mean that they will have a better understanding of important contemporary issues and conflicts that they read and hear about in their daily lives.

In a more general way, students who participate in debate learn how to think critically. Thinking critically does not mean finding fault with things. It means analyzing and synthesizing ideas. Critical thinkers learn to go below the surface of an argument. They learn how to articulate unstated assumptions, and to test the validity of ideas. They learn how ideas relate to each other; they understand the importance of logical consistency. Above all, critical thinkers learn how to think abstractly. They are able to see, through debate, that conflicts are not always about money, or about personal feelings, or about struggles for power—although they may seem to be, on the surface. They learn that conflicts are often animated by differences of values and principles.

> **STUDENTS WHO PARTICIPATE IN DEBATE LEARN HOW TO THINK CRITICALLY**
>
> **THIS IS AN ESSENTIAL SKILL IN MOST OTHER ACTIVITIES**

But critical thinking is not simply a skill that is useful for debate. It is, rather, a general intellectual skill, that is valued in various guises throughout the disciplines that compose a school curriculum. In the study of literature, critical thinkers know that there is more to learning a novel than simply remembering the plot and the names of the main characters. Critical thinkers are able to articulate meanings that lie behind the text; they can see individual works as both the product of an author's vision and an expression of the author's society. In the study of history, critical thinkers do not limit themselves to memorizing facts. They appreciate the movements and forces that shape events. In mathematics and science, critical thinkers see beyond the confines of a particular problem or experiment. They come to understand the structure of laws and axioms.

The thinking skills acquired in debate, then, are important and useful in other activities. And the same may be said for the oratorical skills that are fostered by participation. Debaters learn how to think on their feet, and to express themselves clearly in front of an audience. Those skills can serve them, of course, throughout their academic careers, but they are also fundamentally important in a variety of professions, such as teaching, law or business management. In sum, there are broad educational benefits to participating in debate. Debate is not a closed, isolated skill. Yes, students who participate learn how to debate; but they learn far more as well.

THE COMPOSITION OF A DEBATE CLUB

The foregoing discussion is clearly relevant to the principles guiding the composition of a debate club. Once debate is understood as an activity that is educational and intellectually beneficial, it is clear that it should be offered broadly, not narrowly. In an open society, education does not belong to a privileged minority; it embraces more than just the talented students, or those who can succeed brilliantly. It is axiomatic that the study of mathematics is good for the student who studies hard and struggles to pass, not just for the student who wins the math prize at the end of the year. And it is the same with debate. Some students will win contest after contest, while others will never make it to a final round. But participation in debate is beneficial for all of them, both the winners and the losers.

DEBATE CLUBS SHOULD BE INCLUSIVE NOT EXCLUSIVE

The corollary is that debate clubs should be inclusive, not exclusive. The temptation, in forming any kind of competitive team in a school, is to favor those who will help the team to win; but that kind of favoritism is not appropriate when it excludes students who will gain substantial educational benefits from participating. More than that, the students who are not star debaters can be contributors, not just beneficiaries. As we have emphasized earlier, debate is very much a collaborative activity. Preparation for debate competition involves extensive sharing of ideas in discussions. Students work together to craft cases. It often happens that students who do not do well in competition—because they do not think quickly enough in a spontaneous and reactive context—are major contributors when arguments are constructed beforehand, in the friendly ambiance of the debate clubroom. They can be the students who ask the best questions, or make the subtlest connections. Their participation helps other students to do well in the competition.

FOSTERING A SPIRIT OF INCLUSION AND COOPERATION

Debate clubs work best when there is a strong sense of group identity, when members feel that they are part of something. The individual debater should not feel that he or she is a soloist, meeting casually with other soloists for the sake of a competition, only to go off independently afterwards. The debater should feel, rather, that the debate club is like a symphony orchestra, which exists as an ongoing corporate entity. When that feeling exists, the reward is a broad sense of well-being. When that feeling exists, everyone in the group shares the joy of victory. The disappointment of loss, when shared, is assuaged. A sense of group identity is not a mystical goal that can be achieved only through a lucky combination of people. Rather, it is something that can be created by concrete steps. These steps involve the management of space, the management of time, and the organization of the club structure.

CLUB SPACE

It is important for a debate club to have a home, a room that is largely devoted to the club and its activities. The clubroom should be a place where serious work can be done—where issues can be discussed and speeches written. In that aspect, it should provide resources to debaters: dictionaries, reference books, periodicals—whatever the club's financial support allows. It should also function as the repository of the club's history. It is place to keep records of tournaments, both formal and anecdotal; it is a place to store copies of cases and notes; it is a place to display trophies and pictures. Ideally, the resources should be directly available to the debaters, without the intercession of a coach or teacher.

IT IS IMPORTANT FOR A DEBATE CLUB TO HAVE A HOME

The clubroom should also be a place that permits the casual interaction of students on the team. A sense of camaraderie can be built on the experience of collaborative work, but it also needs an infusion of fun. Friendships cannot be manufactured by decree, of course (although they can certainly be forbidden by decree). They can, however, be encouraged; providing students with a friendly place to meet is one simple step. Debaters should feel, when they go to the debate room, that they are entering a space that belongs to them, where they will find friends who share their enthusiasm for debating.

CLUB MEETINGS AND WORKING SESSIONS

Needless to say, the club space is of little value if there are no activities to fill it. Debate clubs should meet regularly. One model is to have a mandatory weekly meeting for all club members. Even if members are not involved in an upcoming competition (or even if there is no competition in the immediate future), they join together with their partners on the team to find out what issues or events are affecting the team as a whole.

But it should also go without saying, at this point in our handbook, that a significant amount of time must be devoted to regular working sessions. In the sporting world, there are varying practice-to-performance ratios. In some sports, teams practice very little, but play constantly; in other sports, a week of practice will precede a single game. The routine of a good debate team is more like the latter model. Good cases cannot be thrown together at the last minute; they require thinking and discussion. Ideas must be mulled over and distilled; speeches must be drafted and revised. Of course, every school must operate within the constraints of its own schedule, but it should be noted that in some successful programs, debate clubs have working sessions every day of the week, involving at least some of the team members.

Working sessions are devoted, in part, to preparation: that is, to constructing arguments and strategies for a particular competition. But they are also given, in part, to practice. Members of the team spend time debating each other, either with a pending resolution, or with resolutions composed or selected for the occasion. Before going on in our discussion, we would like to emphasize one thing about practice and preparation: here is where most of the education involved in the activity of debate takes place. There is much to be learned in competition as well, but it is really in the day-in and day-out business of practice and preparation that critical thinking skills, and public speaking skills, are developed and honed.

CLUB LEADERSHIP AND ORGANIZATION

In its infancy, a new debate club will depend heavily on the leadership and expertise of adults acting as teachers and coaches. But after programs become established and grow, students themselves can take over many leadership responsibilities. Some successful teams seem almost to be self-perpetuating, although this is only truly possible when they are multigenerational. That is, such teams are not limited to older students, but also include younger ones as well. In well-established programs, the older students joined when they, too, were young. In the last year of their careers as debaters, these students have had three or four years of experience, and have developed some wisdom and expertise with that experience. As 17- or 18-year olds, they meet 14-year old neophytes, who are starting where they started, and must learn what they learned. They are positioned to be effective and sympathetic teachers. In practical terms, that means they can act as judges when younger debaters are practicing; they can watch them compete in actual competitions, and share notes with them afterwards. During preparation sessions, they can work with younger debaters as they craft their cases. What is more, the reverse is also profitable: as they start their careers as debaters, novices can benefit from listening to more seasoned debaters argue. With this kind of organization, team members naturally feel more involved with the organization as a whole. Older members come to take pride in the accomplishments of their younger peers, and feel a sense of responsibility for them, and younger members follow the careers of their mentors with enhanced interest.

The leadership roles described above are broadly shared by the team. In addition, many teams have more carefully defined roles for individuals. In other words, they have students who are elected as president, secretary, treasurer, director of recruitment and orientation, and so forth. The students who fill these roles are not necessarily the most successful debaters in competition. They are students who have shown significant commitment to the well-being of the team. In their various roles, they can be responsible for many of the administrative duties involved in running a team. For example, preparing tournament registrations, keeping club records, collecting dues or travel payments, etc.

RECRUITMENT AND RETENTION

The first task in recruiting members for a debate club is education. Many students (and teachers) simply do not know what debate is. It is essential to inform them. Many people who don't really know about debate think that it is for students who are aggressive or naturally argumentative. They may associate it with slickness of style, rather than solidity of substance. They need to see that debate offers benefits to a broad range of personalities, and draws its inspiration from philosophers, not from smooth-talking politicians. One way to educate the public is to stage a debate demonstration, but that is just a beginning. Students also need to know how the team operates, and what opportunities are available for neophytes. Many students will be attracted by the thrill of competition, and they must be assured that competition is not limited to seasoned veterans. But students should also be educated about the broad intellectual benefits that may be gained from involvement. At its best, a debate program provides an intellectual experience comparable to that offered by the finest academic courses.

In keeping with the principle of inclusion, team leaders must work at keeping debaters on the team. That means providing club members with meaningful activities. If teams rarely compete, or rarely practice, students will quickly lose interest. Teams that rarely practice will rarely win. Students will be quick to desert a losing enterprise. It also means, in some cases, designing special leadership roles for some students; the student who is a perennial loser may become disheartened and think of quitting the club, but will be more likely to stay if given special responsibility for training a cadre of new debaters. It can also help to keep students committed to the team if the club sponsors non-debate events for its members; Ping-Pong matches, basketball games, and entertainment outings can help to build the ties of a permanent community.

Above all, students must understand that the only requirements for club membership are commitment and a willingness to work. Success in competition cannot, and will not, come to every member of the team. Debaters need to know that even if they fail, their places on the team are secure, and their participation is valued.

THE ROLE OF COACHES AND TEACHERS

Any adult who has an abiding concern for the creative education of young people can serve as a debate coach. Coaches do not need to be specialists, with extensive training in oratory or logic (although training is certainly a plus). A debate coach is not expected to pass along a body of knowledge to his or her students, the way that a chemistry teacher might. The rules and procedures of debate that must be taught are comparatively few. The coach's job, actually, is to foster the development of thinking skills in the minds of the debaters. The coach is there to draw things out of the students, rather than to pour things in. The coach must listen, and question, and react. The coach may guide discussions, and give them direction. The coach may help students to focus on the appropriate issues, but should not be regarded as the repository of ultimate truth. Indeed, students need to feel free to disagree with the coach, and to engage with the coach in the same way they would with anyone else involved in the discussion.

The coach must also provide moral leadership for the team. Every member of the team must understand that debaters will behave honestly and ethically in competition. More than that, the coach must set the moral tone for the regular activity of the team. Students will disagree in discussions. If they didn't, the discussions would not be terribly productive. But the coach must ensure that disagreements do not become personal and that comments do not become insulting or demeaning. In discussions, students need to be able to take risks, and to test ideas; they must feel that they can do so without being mocked or disregarded. The coach must create a climate of respect, not simply by offering a model in his or her personal behavior, but by articulating and enforcing standards.

In the classroom, the relationship between students and teachers is sometimes formal and impersonal. Coaching, however, requires a degree of intimate involvement. Coaches must encourage and monitor the development of each debater individually. Practically, that means that coaches must act as judges for intramural debates, and comment on the performance of participants. They must review and criticize written work. And inevitably, coaches become involved with students on a casual basis, and not only on the home turf of the debate room. Participation in a tournament involves a considerable amount of time that is not actually devoted to debating. Many coaches have come to know their students well as they wait in hallways for a round to begin, or for results to be posted.

Coaches have more mundane responsibilities as well. The coach has the ultimate responsibility for managing the internal affairs of the team: its schedule, its membership roster, and its finances. Finances may involve raising money, as well as managing a budget. The coach also must handle its operations on the road: the coach decides who will participate in a given tournament, makes travel arrangements, and handles all the administrative paperwork. Coaches must also recruit and provide the requisite number of judges when the tournament arrives. The coach also serves as a judge personally. It is standard practice that coaches never judge their own debaters, however.

THE ROLE OF PARENTS

Debate offers parents a unique opportunity for involvement in a school activity. Usually, parents are asked to perform the role of spectators at athletic events and artistic performances. In debate, they have the chance to become active participants by serving as judges. Judges do not need to have special expertise. They are meant to be reasonable people. They need simply to be good listeners, and to say who offered them the best argument. Coaches inevitably recruit judges from a wide pool: family members, friends, former debaters, teachers, administrators, etc. It is, by the way, a good idea to involve teachers and administrators as a way to educate the school community. But in many programs, parents form the backbone of the judging pool.

> DEBATE OFFERS PARENTS A UNIQUE OPPORTUNITY FOR INVOLVEMENT IN A SCHOOL ACTIVITY

Parents who don't wish to serve as judges can be involved in other ways. Parents can provide transportation, meals, and even housing to team members when tournaments are underway. They can also serve as spectators, and sources of moral support for their children and their friends. Often, parents value debate not simply because of the benefits it provides their children, but because of the opportunity it offers them to become personally involved, in a supportive way, with their children's education. And sometimes, too, parents form their own communities around debate, which parallel the communities formed by debaters. They also form lasting friendships as a result of the activity.

THE DEBATE CLUB IN THE COMMUNITY OF THE SCHOOL AND BEYOND

We spoke earlier about the importance of educating the school community in the context of recruiting debaters for the team. But even when the team is large and vigorous, education remains important. We assume that when teachers and administrators and students know what debate is, and what it does, they will see it as a valuable activity; it is an educational exercise with extraordinary intellectual merit.

Obviously, the people who actually do it enjoy the benefits of debate most. And yet, there is much to be said for listening to debates as well: spectators often learn a new way of thinking about a problem or an issue. It makes sense, then, to fashion a strong public profile for the debate team: spectators can be invited, both from within the school community, and from outside of it. (For the uninitiated, materials can be prepared which outline the rules and procedures of debate.) As a matter of habit, the debate club should publicize its competitions. Debate resolutions can be announced to the community in advance of the debate. And certainly, the debate club should publicize its results: a team that does well deserves the recognition of the school community. Sometimes this means making use of the school newspaper or announcement system; some clubs, however, also publish their own newsletters.

Chapter 14.
Judging Debates

In the preceding chapters, we focused on debate from the perspective of the students who are participating as debaters. In this chapter, we will focus on the role of the judge.

SUMMARY OBSERVATIONS

Before discussing the specific responsibilities of the judge, we would like to review some of the points about debate made in earlier chapters. First, judges must remember that debate, in the Karl Popper format, is meant to explore and examine significant issues in an even-handed way. As noted in Chapter Three, a good resolution is a debatable proposition. It is something about which reasonable people can and do disagree. If a resolution is well crafted, good arguments can be made in favor of it, and good arguments can be made against it. Debaters, as we have noted, are not like prosecutors and defense attorneys in a criminal court. In a court, there is only one truth possible: the defendant is either guilty or not guilty as charged; the corollary is that the prosecutor and defense attorney cannot both be right. Debaters, however, are not staging a battle of truth and falsehood. They are, rather, illuminating the conflict of values and principles inherent in a resolution. Each side argues for a valid principle. Their conflict centers on the relative importance of those principles in a given context, or it centers on the best way to support those principles.

> **IN THE KARL POPPER FORMAT DEBATE IS MEANT TO EXAMINE AND EXPLORE SIGNIFICANT ISSUES IN AN EVEN-HANDED WAY**

Along these lines, judges must also remember that the burdens of the affirmative and negative teams are equal. In other words, the judge should not assume that the negative position is valid. Unless it is refuted, the validity of the negative position must be established by the arguments of the negative team. And the affirmative team, for its part, cannot confine itself to the refutation of the negative position. It must offer its own reasons for the resolution, independent of what the negative team has said against it.

As the debate progresses, of course, each team does more than simply address the resolution itself. The negative team must argue against the case that the affirmative team has presented, and the affirmative team must argue against the negative case. And then each team, in turn, must defend itself. Affirmative must respond to the criticisms made by the negative team, and negative must respond to the criticisms made by affirmative. Again, the burdens in this regard are equal. Each side must try to refute its opponent; each side must try to rebut its opponent. (For a discussion of these terms, see Chapter Ten.)

In the foregoing chapters, we worked through the individual sections of the debate, and we will not repeat that discussion here. The bottom line, however, is that through all of the argumentative exchanges, through the cross-examinations and refutations and rebuttals, each team has tried to persuade the listeners that its own position is better than the opposing position. The judge must decide which team has done the better job.

> **THE WINNER SHOULD BE THE TEAM WITH THE BEST IDEAS, VALUES, AND ARGUMENTS**

We would also like to reiterate, at this point, that debate in the Karl Popper format is very much a team effort. Although the judge will be asked to award points to individual speakers, the final decision must be based on the performance of the team as a whole. The three debaters on each team are expected to offer an argument that is consistent, cogent and coherent; the judge makes her decision about the persuasiveness of the entire argument. And in this regard, it is really the content of the argument that is of paramount importance. It is true that if the argument is poorly delivered, it will not be easily understood, or persuasive—and we have talked about the relative importance of rhetoric and style in Chapter Twelve. But judges must remember that the essence of debate is the conflict of ideas and values. The winner should be the team with the best ideas, the best values, and the best arguments, even if their opponents have a smoother style and a more impressive manner.

In order to judge a debate, an individual does not need to possess special knowledge or acuity. The judge is supposed to be a reasonable person, not an expert or a sage. Paradoxically, a good judge must try to suppress any special knowledge about the resolution that he or she possesses. Moreover, a good judge must try to suppress personal opinions and feelings. To put it another way, knowledge and opinions must be left at the door of the debating room. The judge is obliged to limit his or her focus to what actually happens in the room, between the two teams that are debating.

> THE JUDGE IS SUPPOSED TO BE A REASONABLE PERSON, NOT AN EXPERT OR A SAGE

We can best explain this, perhaps, with reference to one of the sample resolutions that we have mentioned many times in the preceding chapters. The issue framed by the resolution—that is, the use of official languages in education—is real, not imaginary. Accordingly, most judges will have formed at least some opinions about it before the debate competition even starts. Judges who are coaches, of course, will have pondered the issue extensively while preparing for the competition, and will have even stronger opinions. But in order for the debate to be fair, judges must not let these opinions play a part in their judgment. So even if the judge is convinced that the government must provide education in non-official languages, he must not hold that against the affirmative team. The debaters must debate each other. One of the teams should not have the additional burden of overcoming the silent opposition of the judge.

Now, the foregoing discussion may seem obvious enough. In any kind of a competition, we expect the judges to be impartial and not to show favoritism. The task is a bit harder for debate judges. The judge must also learn not to supply his own silent refutations and rebuttals. Let's say, for the sake of argument, that the affirmative team has presented a constructive that has defined the terms of the resolution unfairly, and has offered a series of logically weak contentions. We will assume that the judge has managed to suppress his own opinions about the resolution—we could even imagine that those submerged opinions were in agreement with the affirmative position. Nonetheless, the judge recognizes that the constructive is weak, and has been listing its faults mentally as he listens. Although he may want to note his objections in his written comments (see below), he cannot let those objections enter into his judgment about the debate. The affirmative team has not broken any rules. A weak argument isn't illegal. A weak argument is, rather, a target for the opposing team. In this scenario, it is the responsibility of the negative team to expose these weaknesses in the course of its cross-examination and refutation. To belabor the obvious: it is the responsibility of the negative team, not the responsibility of the judge. And if the negative team doesn't fulfill this responsibility, the judge cannot do it for them. So it may happen that the affirmative team, with their weak constructive, actually wins the debate: that will happen if they do a good job refuting the negative case, while their own case is left untouched. Yes, it can be frustrating for the judge to see a weak argument survive, but that is the judge's obligation if the weak argument is not attacked. Again, he must limit his focus to what is actually said by the debaters. What he would have said himself is not relevant.

> THE JUDGE'S FOCUS MUST REMAIN ON THE DEBATERS IN THE ROOM AND WHAT THEY ACTUALLY SAY

Along the same lines, judges must refrain from making hypothetical comparisons with debaters that aren't present. A coach who is judging, for example, may think that the affirmative case she is hearing is not as strong as the one put together by her own team, but she must judge the case she hears in the context of the immediate debate. It doesn't matter whether there are better ways to make the argument. What matters is whether the negative case in this round is better. Even a neophyte judge may listen to a contention and think of the refutation that someone made in another round—but other rounds are irrelevant. The judge's focus must remain on the debaters in the room, and on what they actually say.

As we hope we have made clear in the preceding chapters, there is considerable variation in the character of individual debates. As we noted, some debates center on an argument about definitions, some center on an argument about criteria, and some center on arguments about contentions. To put it another way, there is no standard formula for the progress of argument in a debate, even though the format of the round is tightly structured. Sometimes, a critical and decisive moment will come as early as the negative refutation; sometimes, the turning point of the debate will not come until the second affirmative cross-examination. Accordingly, there is no standard formula for judging a debate, which is to say, the judge does not award a precise number of points for each section, and then total them up to find the winner. Neither is the judge's decision based on the debaters' execution of technical minutiae. Debate is not like a competition in figure skating.

THERE IS NO STANDARD FORMULA FOR JUDGING A DEBATE

THE JUDGE'S DECISION SHOULD BE HOLISTIC

The judge's decision, rather, is holistic. The judge must decide which team, on the whole, was more persuasive. Some debates will be close, and the judge will have to weigh a number of disparate factors. It may be that the affirmative team has done a mediocre job of rebutting the negative refutations, but has done a superior job of refuting the negative argument; whereas negative has had a more compelling constructive and has held its ground in cross-examination, but has not answered some affirmative arguments. When the debate is close, it is up to the judge to weigh the relative damage sustained by each side, and to make an appropriate decision. Sometimes, however, debates are not decided on small factors, but on the basis of knockouts, to borrow a term from boxing. Sometimes it happens that the debaters, in the concluding sections of the round, do a good job of boiling down the conflict to one major disagreement. When the debaters work towards such clear voting issues, the judge's role is a bit more straightforward.

As we will discuss in the sections that follow, there are some technical rules involved in debating—relative to timing, the introduction of new arguments, and so on. But these rules rarely figure decisively in judging the debate. A debater cannot be disqualified for being rude, or for exceeding the time limit in cross-examination. When such violations occur, the judge must acknowledge them and give them appropriate weight in making a decision, but there is no automatic penalty process at work.

THE IMPORTANCE OF EXPLANATION The debate judge is not, we would argue, a mere referee, who makes sure that rules are obeyed and infractions are punished. The judge, to use a tautology, must exercise judgment. He must listen carefully, and respond appropriately. Is there, then, a measure of subjectivity in the process? Certainly there is. (If there weren't, there would be no point in having multi-judge panels!) But subjective judgment is not arbitrary. It must be supported by reasons. Moreover, the very fact that judgment is subjective means that it cannot be obscure. In plain terms, judges must explain their reasons for making a certain decision.

JUDGES MUST BE ASSIDUOUS AND THOROUGH IN COMPLETING THEIR BALLOTS

In the context of debate, this means that judges must be assiduous and thorough in completing their ballots. It is not enough merely to say who won. Judges must explain the reason behind their decisions. They should say what they saw as the central issue in the debate. They should point to the aspects of the winning case that made it more persuasive. Likewise, they should identify the shortcomings of the losing side.

Explaining decisions, then, is simply a matter of fairness. It is also, given the purposes of the Karl Popper program, an educational duty. Students are expected to learn when they debate. If they do not know why they have won or lost, they will not have the tools to evaluate their own performance. They will not know what they have done well, or what they need to strengthen.

ETHICAL CONSIDERATIONS Above, we have noted how important it is for the judge to be impartial—that is, to suppress any special knowledge or personal opinions about the resolution when judging the debate. Needless to say, the judge must also be free of any personal inclinations towards the debaters themselves. As noted, coaches should never judge the students from their own teams. The same prohibition applies to parents and volunteers who are representing a school. Even if they do not know the students in the debate round personally, they may find it difficult to vote against their own school when making a decision.

Routinely, of course, coaches come to know students from other schools, and they know the teams that habitually do well in competition against their own students. But that, too, must be left out of consideration when judging a round. It is profoundly unethical for any judge to say that a superior team has lost a round simply because he wants to eliminate that team from the competition and improve the chances of his own team.

The judge's primary responsibility is to decide who wins the round, and to offer reasons for that decision. But the judge has other responsibilities as well. Specifically, the judge must make sure that the round is timed accurately, and that the atmosphere of the debate room is positive.

Affirmative Constructive	6 minutes	Affirmative 1
First Negative Cross-Examination	3 minutes	Affirmative 1 *answers* Negative 3 *asks*
Negative Constructive	6 minutes	Negative 1
First Affirmative Cross-Examination	3 minutes	Affirmative 3 *asks* Negative 1 *answers*
First Affirmative Rebuttal	5 minutes	Affirmative 2
Second Negative Cross-Examination	3 minutes	Affirmative 2 *answers* Negative 1 *asks*
First Negative Rebuttal	5 minutes	Negative 2
Second Affirmative Cross-Examination	3 minutes	Affirmative 1 *asks* Negative 2 *answers*
Second Affirmative Rebuttal	5 minutes	Affirmative 3
Second Negative Rebuttal	5 minutes	Negative 3

Keeping time. In Chapter Two, we included the following structural overview of a round, which indicates the amount of time allotted to each section:

The judge does not need to keep track of time personally. That job can be delegated to a spectator (not, we would emphasize, to a member of either team). Even when the job is delegated, however, the judge must pay attention to the passage of time to make sure that the timekeeping is accurate.

Debaters, of course, must be kept aware of the passage of time as well, and they may stipulate a method to be followed by the timekeeper. Typically, the judge or timekeeper indicates the time remaining in a section by holding up the appropriate number of fingers. Three fingers indicate that three minutes are left, and so on. When only 30 seconds are left, the timekeeper indicates this by closing the hand halfway. When time is exhausted, the timekeeper forms a fist. It is not necessary, by the way, for the fingers to be held aloft constantly: it is only necessary that the speaker be aware of the transitional milestones. If the speaker doesn't look in the right direction when the change is made, the fingers must be held up until he sees them.

It is understood that when the stop signal is given, the speaker will not stop in mid-sentence. It is perfectly acceptable for the speaker to complete a sentence or a thought. But the speaker is not free to simply disregard the signal. If she begins a new point, or a new train of thought, the judge should ignore what she says, and should not take it into account in making a decision. If a team habitually overruns time limits, the judge should certainly note this on the ballot, and may weigh it as a factor in making a decision. In cross-examination, it is customary to allow the respondent time to finish his answer, but the questioner may not ask a new question. If the stop signal comes in the middle of a question, the cross-examination ends at that point, with the question unanswered.

Preparation time must also be carefully tracked. As noted in Chapter Five, preparation time is taken at the discretion of the debaters. Each team has eight minutes; they take as much of that as want at intervals of their own choosing. The timekeeper must keep a running account of this time as it is taken, so that it is clear to the debaters how much time they have used, and how much time they have left. Typically, debaters will announce that they want to use time before they use it, but this is not required. The timekeeper must pay attention and start counting off time if the debaters are sitting down to write or confer, even if they have not announced their intention. Some debaters will announce that they intend to take a specific amount of time, but this should be regarded as a gesture of courtesy, not a contract. If the debater says two minutes, but takes three, or only one, it is still the amount of time actually used that must be recorded.

Because debaters are usually writing or talking during prep time, hand signals are ineffi-cient. Usually, the timekeeper will announce the passage of time verbally, at intervals of thirty seconds. Rarely, a team will continue to prepare after the eight minutes of time have been exhausted; in such a case, the additional time used must be deducted from the team's final speech. Tactically, this is most unwise—which explains why it is rare for debaters to exceed their allotted preparation time

DURING A
DEBATE
THE JUDGE MUST
BE ENCOURAGING
AND SUPPORTIVE
RATHER THAN
THREATENING

Maintaining a positive atmosphere: Generally, the judge should not inter-vene with the debaters as the debate progresses. It is, however, the judge's responsibil-ity to ensure that the spectators do not interfere with the debate. Because debate requires intense concentration, the debaters should not have to deal with distractions, such as spectators talking. And, of course, debaters should not have deal with any active forms of disruption. The judge must take steps to reprimand or expel any spectators who are disruptive.

The judge can also do much to establish a positive atmosphere at the beginning of the round. It is expected that debaters will treat each other with respect, and will conduct their debate in a friendly, nonconfrontational manner. If the judge treats the debaters in a friendly manner, the debaters are likely to follow her lead.

During the debate, the judge must assume a manner that is encouraging and supportive, rather than threatening. Speakers can easily get rattled if judges make non-verbal signs of disapproval. Judges should not frown or shake their heads if they disagree with a point. Even positive signs, such as smiling and nodding, can be disconcerting—not for the speaker, perhaps, but for his opponents who are watching. By sending such signals—either negative or positive—the judge is inserting herself into the action of the debate. As we argued above, the conflict should take place between the teams, not between the debaters and the judge.

RULES OF PROCEDURE

Judging a debate involves more than following a rulebook. The judge's task is to decide which team offers a better argument, and no rulebook can offer a way to measure the strength of an argument. Nonetheless, there are some general rules of procedure in the Karl Popper format, and judges should be aware of them as they make their decisions.

SILENCE MEANS CONSENT

In chapters seven through eleven, we described in some detail the various purposes of each section of the round. Here, we will summarize the rules of procedure that were touched on in that discussion. One general principle, that runs through all of these sections, is that silence means consent. So, for instance, if the negative team does not challenge the affirmative definitions, those definitions are assumed to be acceptable to both sides. Or if negative makes a refutation of an affirmative point, and affirmative does not respond to that refutation, it is assumed that the refutation is conceded to be true.

Affirmative Constructive
In this section, the affirmative team is expected to offer its complete argument in favor of the resolution. Although they may repeat points and expand on them in later sections of the debate, they may not introduce a new criterion, new contentions, or new definitions at a later time. The affirmative speaker may read this speech from a manuscript, or may speak from notes; either is acceptable.

First Negative Cross-Examination
The two debaters are expected to face the audience, rather than each other. The negative debater is supposed to ask questions, rather than make speeches. The affirmative debater is supposed to answer those questions; she should not make speeches, or ask questions in return. The affirmative debater during this cross-examination may make concessions, but it is incumbent upon the negative team to capitalize on these concessions in the speech that follows. (In other words, the judge is not expected to see the significance of such concessions on his own.)

Negative Constructive and Refutation
Like the affirmative team in its constructive, the negative team is expected to offer a complete argument against the resolution. It must also begin its task of refuting the affirmative argument. If affirmative's definitions are not challenged at this point, they must stand. Similarly, if negative does not offer a competing criterion, it is assumed that the criterion articulated by the affirmative team will govern the round. Finally, the negative team must challenge affirmative contentions, if only in outline form; otherwise, it is assumed that they are acceptable. (The order of these tasks is at the discretion of the speaker; some speakers will present the constructive argument first, before moving on to the refutation; some speakers prefer to handle the refutation first.)

First Affirmative Cross-Examination
The rules of procedure outlined above for the first negative cross-examination also apply here.

First Affirmative Rebuttal

The affirmative speaker has two tasks in this speech. First, she must outline her team's refutations of the negative argument. Second, she must respond to the refutations made by the negative team (that is, their objections to the affirmative case). In this section, the general principle articulated above is in full force. If the affirmative speaker does not refute a given point in the negative case, then that point stands; if the affirmative speaker does not respond to a particular negative objection, then that objection is conceded. (The order of these tasks is at the discretion of the speaker: she may refute first and rebut later, or do it the other way around.)

Second Negative Cross-Examination

The rules of procedure outlined above for the first negative cross-examination also apply here.

First Negative Rebuttal

As with the affirmative rebuttal described above, the negative speaker has a dual task. First, he must respond to the refutations made by the affirmative. Second, he must continue to attack the affirmative case. At this point in the debate, the negative speaker may start to draw the judge's attention to points that have been dropped. That is, he will indicate items in the negative refutation to which affirmative has not responded. Such a dropped point is treated as a concession made by the affirmative team. The negative speaker is not allowed to introduce completely new arguments at this point; previous arguments, however, may be revised, rephrased, or expanded.

Second Affirmative Cross-Examination

The rules of procedure outlined above for first negative cross-examination also apply here.

Second Affirmative Rebuttal

The task of the affirmative speaker is reactive. She must renew refutations that have not been addressed adequately. Usually, this means pointing out flaws in the negative rebuttal. She must rebut refutations that have been kept alive by negative in its last speech. At this point, most good debaters will deliberately let some points drop, and will focus the judge's attention on the key issues of the round. The speaker may or may not instruct the judge; that is, the speaker may or may not articulate a standard of judgment for the round.

Second Negative Rebuttal

In essence, the second negative rebuttal is similar to the second affirmative rebuttal. Judges must be especially wary of speakers introducing new arguments at this point. Of course, a new argument would have been illegal in the first rebuttal made earlier; an illegal argument made at that point, however, could have been flagged by the affirmative team in its rebuttal. Now, the affirmative ream has no chance to respond, so a new argument is especially unfair. The judge must ignore any new arguments that are introduced.

TAKING NOTES

JUDGES MUST TAKE NOTES DURING A DEBATE

By this point, it probably goes without saying that judges must take notes during the debate. Without notes, it is all but impossible to keep track of the refutations and rebuttals as they are made. Most judges follow the same routine as the debaters. They flow the debate on a pad of paper that is divided into columns. One column is given to each section of the debate. In outline form, the judge can note the contentions made in the affirmative constructive in one column; in an adjacent column, he can list the refutations made by the negative in its following speech, and draw links between the two. It is possible, with a good flow, to follow a line of argument through an entire debate.

If judges keep accurate notes, they can see for themselves whether or not points have been dropped and conceded. Without notes, they are at the mercy of the debaters, who will sometimes interpret the progress of the debate to suit their own purposes. Only a judge who has paid close attention and made careful notes will see that some instructions are somewhat skewed.

We should also, in this context, make a few observations about dropping points. Debaters, naturally, like to focus the judge's attention on such drops; but judges should remember that a dropped point does not automatically determine the winner of the debate. Rather, the judge must weigh the significance of the point, or points, that have been dropped. As we know from military history, it is quite possible to lose a number of battles—but still win a war.

WRITING BALLOTS

Earlier in this chapter, we discussed the importance of writing down the reasons that support a judge's decision. When they do not know the reasons why they won or lost, debaters have little opportunity to learn from the experience. Communicating these reasons is the judge's primary task in writing a ballot. On the ballot, the judge can identify arguments that seemed especially strong or weak. She can also address specific aspects of the debate (e.g., she might say that the negative cross-examination was especially good, or that the affirmative rebuttal seemed confused. The ballot also gives the judge a chance to address matters of style and performance. Judges can note if a speaker was inaudible, or overly aggressive, or rude. Judges can use points to determine a speaker's position in a debate round. Points are a reward for the speaker, but do not determine the final outcome of the round.

GIVING REASONS FOR DECISIONS IS THE JUDGE'S PRIMARY TASK IN WRITING A BALLOT

When writing comments, judges need to remember that debating is difficult for most debaters; debaters can feel sensitive or insecure—even if they win the round. It is important, then, for comments to be supportive and understanding. There is a world of difference between writing, "your second contention was stupid" and writing "your second contention was unclear, and did not seem consistent with your first."

DISCLOSING RESULTS

In all competitions, judges are expected to come to their decisions independently, without any discussion—either with other judges (if there is a panel) or with the debaters themselves. In some competitions, judges are forbidden to make verbal comments to the debaters; all commentary must be confined to the ballot. In other competitions, however, judges are encouraged to talk with the debaters, after they have made their decisions. Such discussions can be very helpful to debaters, because they allow judge to explain things at greater length. Verbal comments, however, should be used to amplify written comments, rather than replace them. After all, comments are useful not simply to the debaters themselves, but to the coaches who have prepared them; the coach will not be in the debate room to hear the judge's comments. Therefore, a written record on the ballot is essential.

THE KARL POPPER DEBATE FORMAT ENCOURAGES THE DISCLOSURE OF RESULTS

In competitions where verbal comments are encouraged, it is only natural for the judge to disclose the decision in the course of those comments. Without knowing the decision, debaters have no context within which to place comments; only when they know the winner and the loser can they appreciate the strength or weakness of a given argument that the judge is criticizing. In the Karl Popper Debate Format, judges are encouraged to explain their decision as fully as possible in order to enhance the educational value of debate.

The transcript below is of an actual debate that took place in 1997. The debaters are not native English speakers. The transcript has been edited for clarity, but every effort has been made to maintain the spirit of the original debaters' arguments.

RESOLUTION: SOFT DRUGS SHOULD BE LEGALIZED

FIRST AFFIRMATIVE: MARTINA

MARTINA: Opponents, judges, members of the audience, my name is Martina. I would like to present my team. Ema is the second speaker and Tamara will speak third. Today we will debate the issue of legalizing soft drugs. First, I would like to present our definitions. Soft drugs are derivatives of cannabis, and what we are talking about today are marijuana and hashish. According to the *Oxford English Dictionary*, legalization means making something allowed or required by law. Another thing has to be mentioned, legalization does not mean that soft drugs will be available to all. Any person wishing to buy soft drugs will be required to show identification, sales to minor will not be permitted.

Another thing is very important, and I hope that you will recognize it in all of our arguments, and that is our criterion. Our criterion is the good of the community. The question of whether to legalize soft drugs is a controversial and much discussed topic. When we were discussing it, we came to the conclusion that prejudice and cultural bias inform much of the public discourse around legalization, rather than facts. Surprisingly, many people don't realize that soft drugs are less harmful than, for example, cigarettes or alcohol. There is a double standard in our society, and we want to see it eliminated.

We will start with our first argument: the right to free choice. The right to free choice is a fundamental human right. I hope you recognize the importance of this right. It is the basis for democratic society. A democratic society treats its citizens as rational beings and gives them the right to make their own decisions. If we take that right away, we make them subjects, not citizens. This is something that we want to avoid. If we allow the state to interfere with our rights, it must only be under special circumstances, and soft drug use is not one of them. Why? There are two reasons. First, users of soft drugs

COMMENTARY ON THE AFFIRMATIVE

INTRODUCTION: *Martina's introductory remarks could be stronger. She has stated the topic of the resolution, but she has not stated the resolution itself. We know that the resolution concerns the legalization of soft drugs, but we don't know what side she is on. Even though it is late in the competition, and we can presume that everyone knows what the resolution is, she should still state the resolution and her team's position explicitly. Her opening remarks would also be stronger with a contextual introduction. She might have used a quote to highlight her criterion ("the good of the community"), or her first argument ("the right to free choice"). As it stands, she jumps right in without first suggesting why the issue is important.*

DEFINITION OF TERMS: *Martina offers a clear and fair definition of soft drugs. She has made it clear what the affirmative team intends to argue about. Her definition of legalization, however, could be more precise. She notes that it "means making something allowed or required by law." Allowing and requiring are two different things, however. Her argument shows that she means the former, and she should say so clearly now. She also offers a qualification of the meaning of legalization: namely, that legalization does not mean unlimited free access; even legal substances can be restricted to keep them away from younger citizens. This is a fair qualification, but it would be better if she made it clear this is part of her understanding of the word legalization. As it is, it sounds as if she is describing how her position would be put into practice.*

ARTICULATION OF THE CRITERION: *In her constructive speech, Martina designates "the good of the community" as the criterion for the affirmative case. This is a good example of a criterion that could be more precisely defined. Society benefits from many things: security, peace, economic prosperity, and so on. It is not clear exactly which social benefits will be maximized, or how they can be measured. Indeed, as the negative team will argue, the good of society as a whole seems to fit more naturally with the negative position.*

Martina follows her articulation of the criterion with some general remarks about society's ignorance of the facts about soft drugs, and a charge that there is a double standard in the restriction of drugs, since they are "less harmful than, for example, cigarettes or alcohol," which are legal. The implicit admission that drugs are harmful will cause her difficulties in cross-examination. It would have been better to avoid this admission. Again, we note the importance of writing out the constructive speech in full before the debate. It is far easier to see and eliminate potentially damaging remarks from a text than from an outline.

ARGUMENTS: *Martina's first argument is the right to free choice, which she describes as one of the fundamental human rights. This is a reasonable argument, and fits well with the affirmative position, that citizens should be free to choose to take drugs. The difficulty here is that it does not connect directly to the criterion that she articulated. In fact, there is a natural conflict between individual freedom of choice and the good of society as whole. The two ideas can be reconciled, but Martina does not make the relationship between them clear. She suggests, in a general way, that if every one in society has free choice, then society itself will be better off. Ultimately, however, this logic is circular. If every one in society has free choice, then society itself will be better, because it is good to have free choice (see our discussion of begging the question in Chapter Five).*

It would have made more sense to have offered individual liberty as the criterion. According to John Stuart Mill, individual freedom is the primary value in society, and should be restricted only to preserve the individual freedom of others. Martina makes this point as she develops her argument, but she misses the corollary, which is that "the good of the community" as a whole is of secondary importance, at best, and should not shape the construction of laws.

do not jeopardize anybody else's rights. This is very important. Second, the use of soft drugs is not harmful enough to call for state intervention, which is itself a greater danger. We will demonstrate this later.

Our second argument concerns the pragmatic benefits of legalization. There are two aspects to this argument: benefits to the individual and benefits to the community. The benefits to the individual are quality control, which reduces the harm associated with soft drugs—remember that, it is very important. Other benefits to the individual concern price control and the "forbidden fruit" effect. I hope that you are all familiar with this concept. Some things become more appealing simply because they are forbidden, and this is one of the reasons young people use drugs. So by legalization, we would actually eliminate one of reasons for using drugs.

Regarding benefits to the community. First I must mention taxes and the reallocation of resources—they are connected, which is why I mention them together. The additional taxes generated by the legalization of soft drugs would put more cash in the state register. More cash in the state register means more cash for other things that are more important than enforcing the prohibition against soft drugs. What does it mean specifically? It means we can invest in pursuing hard drugs, which is extremely important. We can invest in education, we can invest in health care, and many other things. Later on in this debate we will present concrete examples.

I have to say something about other benefits to the community: demystification and destigmatization. Again, they are connected. Legalization will bring demystification, and that will allow society to talk openly about soft drugs, and stop moralizing. We will be free to talk about drug use, we will be free to get information. We will know what we are dealing with. We will be able to recognize the real problem, and then we will be better equipped to solve it. Regarding destigmatization—I said that they were connected—it means that people who use soft drugs will no longer be treated as criminals.

I have to mention one more thing and that is the effect of legalization on the black market, which we find extremely important. What does this mean? Most importantly, it means a separation of the market for soft drugs from the market for hard drugs. Finally, the only thing I can say is that soft drugs are not forbidden because they are dangerous. They are dangerous because they are forbidden. It is extremely important to recognize this, and therefore I beg you to think about it. Thank you.

CROSS-EXAMINATION OF THE FIRST AFFIRMATIVE (MARTINA) BY THE THIRD NEGATIVE (IVA)

IVA: Okay, hello Martina. When you are driving in a car, do you put on a seatbelt?

MARTINA: Sometimes I do and sometimes I don't.

IVA: So when you do put it on, why do you put it on?

MARTINA: To protect myself.

IVA: Okay, and tell me, the fact that you're obliged by the law to put on a seatbelt, do you consider this to be normal?

MARTINA: No, not really.

IVA: Not really. Okay, well tell me, you were talking about prejudices and how people have prejudices connected with drugs. What sort of opinion will be created if we do legalize soft drugs? What will people then think about drugs?

MARTINA: People will realize that drugs are not as dangerous as they believe they are, and they will accept them, as they did alcohol and cigarettes.

IVA: So people will accept drugs. Do you think this is good for the community?

Before going on to her second argument, Martina repeats her admission that soft drugs are harmful. She also contends that the restriction of drugs is extremely dangerous, but does not say why, although she promises that this will be explained later. This is not a wise strategy. The affirmative is supposed to present a full case in the constructive speech. It is hardly persuasive or compelling to say that an argument will be explained later. The negative team in cross-examination will exploit both of these matters.

Martina's second argument about "pragmatic benefits" is split into two subsections, the benefits to the individual and benefits to the community. She lists three benefits to the individual: quality control, price control, and the forbidden fruit effect. She does not explain price control at all. Her brief reference to quality control says that it would influence harm—this suggests that poor quality drugs, that cause harm, would be eliminated. She gives a fuller explanation of the forbidden fruit effect. In short, if drugs are legalized, then fewer people will want to take them. This is not a strong argument at all. The implication is that society will benefit if drug use is reduced (and this should be taken in tandem with the earlier admission that drugs are harmful). This forces the affirmative team to make the paradoxical argument that the best way to reduce drug use is to legalize drugs. They have also opened a very wide door for the negative team. They have said that society will benefit (this, remember, the criterion) if drug use is reduced. The negative team can win by showing that prohibition is a better way of reducing drug use than legalization is.

The pragmatic benefits outlined for the community are somewhat stronger—but are still, as we will see, vulnerable to negative attack. The first benefit to the community is financial. It is implied that there will be a tax on newly legalized soft drugs, and that the community will benefit from increased tax revenue. The second benefit, however, is logically circular. Martina talks about demystification and destigmatization, but the essence of the point is decriminalization. The logic is that if drugs are made legal, then the people who use them will no longer be doing something illegal. Martina concludes by saying that illegal sales of drugs on the black market will be reduced—again, because soft drugs will no longer be illegal. This point, too, is circular, but that may be because her discussion of it is incomplete. It would be stronger, for example, to say that the revenues of drug dealers would be reduced that contact between hard drug dealers and soft drug users would be eliminated.

Martina ends her speech with a neat rhetorical flourish, by saying that soft drugs are not illegal because they are dangerous, but are dangerous because they are illegal. This statement does not really sum up the affirmative case, however, and her presentation would be stronger if she had concluded by restating, in summary form, the main arguments of the affirmative case.

COMMENTARY ON THE FIRST AFFIRMATIVE CROSS-EXAMINATION

Iva begins her questioning by trying to gain a concession that will be helpful for her case. Martina has argued that the state is permitted to interfere with the individual only when that individual is jeopardizing someone else's rights. She brings up the seatbelt law to show that the state sometimes acts to prevent injuries that individuals can do to themselves (instead of to others). She asks Martina if the law requiring seatbelt use is "normal." Martina rejects the law, which is the danger of this line of questioning. Martina, in effect, does not make the desired concession, but her refusal does not seem unreasonable.

Iva goes on to clarify some of the points in Martina's constructive speech. She gets Martina to say, even more clearly than before, that the acceptance of drug use as part of society will benefit society. In the course of her answer, Martina repeats a phrase from

MARTINA: Yes, I do.

IVA: You think that a society in which drug use is considered to be normal is good?

MARTINA: Yes I do because drugs are normal, and they already are a part of society.

IVA: But just because people are using them, does that make them normal?

MARTINA: No it doesn't, but another thing does. They are not harmful enough. We accept a lot of different things. Why shouldn't we accept drug use?

IVA: Okay I would like to discuss this term, "harmful enough." What exactly does "harmful enough" mean?

MARTINA: We will give you that information, but I can tell you, it means that they do not endanger anybody's life, or anybody else's rights.

IVA: Okay so things like lung cancer and toxic psychosis are not dangerous enough?

MARTINA: Yes they are, but soft drugs are not the only thing that can cause that, cigarettes can cause lung cancer. You can get lung cancer just like that, from many things. It is not directly connected with soft drugs.

IVA: Okay, so what you are saying is we don't have enough bad things in society right now so we could use another one as well? Like we have alcohol and cigarettes, why shouldn't we have soft drugs?

MARTINA: No, what I am saying is let's give people a right to decide.

IVA: Okay, you are saying that banning soft drugs is extremely dangerous, those were your exact words.

MARTINA: Yes

IVA: Soft drugs are currently banned in all democratic countries except for the Netherlands. How is that extremely dangerous? What dangerous things have happened in the United States or other Western countries where drugs are currently banned?

MARTINA: You mentioned Holland, it is one example, but it is the only example and it is the example that actually shows some positive effects.

IVA: No, no, no, I'm talking about other countries where drugs are banned. What is so extremely dangerous, because you used the phrase "extremely dangerous," that is happening in countries where drugs are banned?

MARTINA: Well, what if, for example, the state decides that some books, or some information is dangerous. Would you let the state decide that for you?

IVA: Okay.

MARTINA: This is dangerous. What is going on in that case?

IVA: I would like to continue this conversation, but since our time is up, thank you.

MARTINA: Thank you.

FIRST NEGATIVE (LUKA)

LUKA: Choose life, choose family, and choose a career. This is the response of the negative team: Luka, Katarina, and Iva. The dilemma is whether soft drugs should be legalized or not. We will provide a firm negative case that will show that drugs should not be legalized and we will refute the affirmative arguments. First, we will accept the affirmative criterion, which is the good of the community. Why? Because we believe that negative's arguments better support this criterion than the affirmative arguments. We have two arguments. The first is that soft drugs are harmful to the individual and the second argument is that soft drugs are harmful to society.

Regarding harms to the individual, these include both physiological harms and psychological harms. We will hear more evidence about this in the second speech, but suffice it to say for now that the physiological harms of soft drugs are short term memory loss, an impaired ability to learn, lung damage, heart damage, and damage to the reproductive her constructive, saying that soft drugs are not "harmful enough," and Iva demands a clarification of that expression. Martina does not give a definition, although she promises that her team will do so later (they don't), and tries to steer her answer back to an assertion that drugs affect no one but the user. Iva pursues a new line of questioning, about the physical harm done by drugs, and Martina admits that drugs are physically harmful, but counters that other substances, which are legal, are also harmful. Iva presses this point—but a little too hard. She tries to get Martina to say that her position is that it doesn't matter how many bad things there are in society, and Martina (naturally) denies saying that. She has the chance to reiterate, instead, the importance of free choice.

Finally, Iva pursues Martina's statement in the constructive that the banning of drugs is "extremely dangerous." Martina did not explain this. Iva's questioning makes it clear that Martina has invoked the "slippery slope" argument: that if drugs are banned, other liberties will also be banned (see Chapter Five). As negative will show later, the problem with this argument, logically, is that banning drugs is already the status quo—and that civil liberties are robust in countries that ban soft drugs.

In sum, Iva has clarified some of the points of Martina's constructive, to damaging effect. She highlighted affirmative's admission that soft drugs are harmful, and she has tried to win a concession for her side, that the state is justified in restricting harmful substances.

COMMENTARY ON THE NEGATIVE CONSTRUCTIVE AND REFUTATION

In Chapter Nine, we discussed the strategic choices that must be made by the negative team at this point. They can choose to challenge the affirmative team at the level of definitions, at the level of the criterion, and at the level of the arguments. In this debate, the negative team does not challenge the affirmative definitions; since the definitions were fair and neutral, that is an appropriate decision. They also decide to accept the affirmative criterion, "the good of the community." This, too, is appropriate; as we noted above, and as Luka remarks in this speech, this criterion fits better with the negative side of the resolution than it does with the affirmative side. Luka does not, however, explain exactly what is meant by the good of the community—the phrase remains vague. In any case, the strategy for the debate has been set. The negative team will try to prove that society benefits from the ban on soft drugs.

system. Soft drugs also affect motor abilities, and this can cause dysfunctional behaviors in society, for example, driving while under the influence of soft drugs.

The second subpoint of this first argument concerns the psychological, ladies and gentlemen. Soft drugs are psychoactive, meaning they affect our behavior, the way we feel, and the way we think. For these reasons, we cannot allow soft drugs to be legalized. They cause toxic psychosis, panic, anxiety, flashbacks, and can increase the likelihood of mental illness in some individuals.

Our second argument is that soft drugs are harmful to society. To begin with, we must say that the affirmative side is promoting a sort of escapism. How? By deliberately getting high, people avoid reality. And we believe that by getting high, they are getting low, because they cannot function normally in society. In our second speech we will talk about the effectiveness of laws banning drug use.

The second subpoint of our second argument is that we want citizens to have an active role in society. Actually, we want responsible citizens. The affirmative side talked about freedom, but we say that freedom has two faces. The other face is responsibility. If we are not responsible, we cannot be free. The third subpoint is that the goal of the affirmative team is primarily egotistical. Soft drugs are currently available for medicinal purposes. But many use them simply to get high, and this benefits no one. And I repeat, the good of the community is the criterion for this debate. Getting high benefits no one. It harms all.

Affirmative talked about prejudices and facts, saying that facts show that alcohol and cigarettes are more harmful than soft drugs. We have heard no evidence to support this. They spoke of a double standard. Ladies and gentlemen, there are universals for what is wrong. Soft drugs are wrong and must not be legalized. Even if alcohol and cigarettes are as harmful, or more harmful, this does not justify the legalization of soft drugs. This would simply create a third legalized harm.

Affirmative's first argument concerned the right to free choice. But free choice isn't unlimited. The state has the right to limit choice. Article 16 of the Croatian constitution says that rights and freedom can be limited if citizens' health or public morality are endangered. Affirmative was speaking about freedom. Freedom means responsibility. They say that we are rational beings, rational beings must be responsible to the state and to the laws. Citizens cannot abuse their freedom of choice in order to destroy themselves or others. The state has the right to protect them from themselves and to protect others.

What risk do we face by prohibiting soft drugs? Affirmative alluded to some risk in their first speech. But there is no risk. America is a democratic country, soft drugs are banned there, but they do not suffer because of this. The Nazis are not in power. Democrats are in power. There is no risk to that democracy because soft drugs are banned. And are soft drugs harmful or not? And what does "harmful enough" mean? And who has the right to choose what is harmful enough? Ladies and gentlemen, the state has the right. Therefore, the state has the right to protect citizens and to ban soft drugs.

Affirmative's second argument was the forbidden fruit effect. We can draw an analogy with theft. If we make theft legal, then we can expect more theft, because thieves will go unpunished. The same thing will happen with soft drugs. If we make them available, then we will see an increase not a decrease in the use of soft drugs. As to price controls, making something bad less expensive and more available isn't a good thing. Lowering prices causes more consumption, and more consumption is bad. Likewise with quality control. Soft drugs generally aren't of high quality.

At first, the negative case seems as misdirected as the affirmative. The affirmative team articulated the criterion of social benefits, and then began arguing about the individual's right to choose. Here, the negative team uses the same criterion, and it, too, begins by talking about the harm done to the individual. Although negative might have made the link to the criterion more specific, their argument is logically sound. The assertion that harm is done to individuals is actually a minor premise in a syllogistic argument: drugs damage the capabilities of individuals; because they are not as capable as they might be, drug users do not make contributions to society; therefore, society suffers from the consequences of drug use. The corollary, of course, is that society benefits when drug use is reduced. The argument is vulnerable to the extent that the premises can be refuted. It falls apart if it can be established that drug users, as a group, do not stop making contributions to society.

One flaw in Luka's presentation is that, like his counterpart on the affirmative team, he has promised that part of the negative case will be delivered at a later time, in the next speech. As a matter of form, the entire case should be laid out at this time, even if it is amplified in the course of making rebuttals later on. Other flaws are structural. Although the first argument is broken down into subpoints in a reasonable way (distinguishing between the physical and psychological effects of drug use), the breakdown of the second argument is less successful. Indeed, the third subpoint refers explicitly to the affirmative case (as in a refutation), even though Luka is supposed to be explaining the negative case on its own terms.

Luka makes a number of strong points in the refutation part of the speech. The only real difficulties here are, again, structural. He begins by challenging the importance of free choice, articulated by the affirmative team in their first argument. He counters that individual choice is usually limited in some way, and can be limited to prevent harm to the self as well as harm to others. But then he modulates into an attack on the slippery slope argument made by the affirmative—although this was mentioned briefly in the context of their first point, it was not made explicit until cross-examination, and he should make that clear. His attack on the second argument of the affirmative case is clearer. In fact, he explains the concept of price control, when the affirmative team didn't. His refutation here makes sense. There is nothing beneficial about lowering the price of something bad. With regard to quality control, there is no way to create quality in a bad product. His forbidden fruit analogy could be clearer, however. The affirmative team has argued, in essence, that the ban on drugs makes them attractive. The negative team's response is that the ban, and the fear of punishment, act as deterrents. What Luka fails to exploit is the implication of the forbidden fruit argument itself—the affirmative team has argued that after legalization, drug use will decrease, and society will benefit from decreased drug use. Luka touches very quickly on the hypocrisy of the state

Affirmative also talked about benefits to the community. They mentioned increased tax revenues, but it is hypocritical for the state to make money by harming citizens' health. Regarding the black market, legalization will allow criminals who already monopolize the drug market to make even more money. Affirmative says it would be good for the community if the use of soft drugs were considered normal. But we must consider such usage unnormal and unbeneficial and let it be banned. Affirmative said in cross-examination that the state doesn't have the right to restrict. Ladies and gentlemen, the state has the duty to make some things legal and others illegal. Soft drugs must be illegal. If we are not responsible, we cannot be free. And we cannot be free to choose the harm that soft drugs cause. Thank you very much.

CROSS-EXAMINATION OF FIRST NEGATIVE (LUKA) BY THIRD AFFIRMATIVE (TAMARA)

TAMARA: Okay Luka, I have a few questions for you. First of all, do you consider yourself to be a more or less rational being?

LUKE: Well, a more rational being.

TAMARA: A more rational being, okay. Do you think that because of that you are able to make decisions for yourself?

LUKA: Well, some decisions.

TAMARA: Okay, great. Do you want the state that you live in to recognize you as a rational being who can make decisions for himself?

LUKA: Well, that would be nice.

TAMARA: Yes, okay great. You said something about how the state has the right to limit everything that is unhealthy for a person.

LUKA: No, I didn't say that, I said it has the right to limit everything that is very harmful for citizens.

TAMARA: Very harmful.

LUKA: Yes.

TAMARA: Can you define very harmful, since you say we can't?

LUKA: Well, I think that affirmative team has to give the definitions.

TAMARA: Okay, tell me, does the state have the right to say how much candy you can eat?

LUKA: Can you say that again?

TAMARA: Does the state have the right to say how much candy you can eat?

LUKA: Well, if candy is carcinogenic, yes.

TAMARA: Okay, do you think that the state has the right to say, for example, how much television you can watch?

LUKA: Well, the same answer. Yes, if watching television is very harmful, deadly, or very unhealthy.

TAMARA: Okay, deadly or very unhealthy?

LUKA: Okay.

TAMARA: Okay thank you. Tell me, do you know of a case in which somebody died from using soft drugs?

LUKA: Well, people often use drugs and they go on to do bad things under the influence.

TAMARA: Okay, but do you know of a case, a specific case, of somebody dying because they used soft drugs?

LUKA: Well, among my friends, no, but I am sure that—

TAMARA: So, you have never heard of such a case, in all your research?

making money on harmful activities. The end of his speech is rather hurried, as he tries to say what was established in cross-examination. Essentially, he repeats some of the things that Martina has said, and simply contradicts them, without disproving them. He would have done better to highlight the slippery slope fallacy that was exposed in cross-examination, and the importance of affirmative's admission that drugs are harmful.

COMMENTARY ON THE FIRST NEGATIVE CROSS-EXAMINATION

In this exchange, Tamara begins by trying to re-establish the importance of individual freedom, and asks Luka a series of leading questions about his role as a rational being functioning in a state. She wants Luka to admit that he wants to make choices for himself. Luka qualifies most of his answers. Then, she hopes to establish that there is a contradiction between wanting to make choices, and allowing the state to interfere with those choices. Luka insists, however, that the state's interference is allowable only when individual choices would lead to something "very harmful." Logically, Luka's position is sound; he does not serve himself well, however, by refusing to explain terms that he has introduced himself. It is not the responsibility of the affirmative team to define terms introduced by the negative team.

In response to Tamara's questioning, Luka asserts that "very harmful" means "deadly or very unhealthy." Tamara seeks to exploit this explanation by asking for evidence that the use of soft drugs causes death. Although her questioning is very aggressive, it is tactically flawed. She has framed her questions in the hopes that Luka will admit that there has never been a single case of someone dying because of the use of soft drugs. It is easy for Luka to assert that deaths have resulted from drug use. In other words, he has kept Tamara from establishing her position that soft drugs are not deadly.

Again, Tamara is aggressive in demanding specifics about the effects of drug use. She offers a series of hypothetical responses, which are meant to establish that the effects are minimal. Although these questions may be rhetorically effective, they are not tactically sound. When she asks Luka if a person under the influence of drugs might steal, he is certainly not going to say no—and if he says yes, she has lost the point she was trying to make. After another needlessly aggressive gesture—asking Luka to define a word for her, a word that he has not used—she concludes her questioning by trying to clarify the extent of the state's power over individuals. The exchange is confusing, in that Luka

LUKE: I have heard—

TAMARA: You've heard of such a case?

LUKA: Yes, I've heard of numerous car crashes caused by the driver's use of soft drugs.

TAMARA: Okay, can you give me the data on how soft drugs can influence behavior, because you said they influence human behavior, but you didn't specify exactly how. So, can you specify now?

LUKA: Marijuana is a psychoactive drug.

TAMARA: Okay.

LUKA: So, it changes—

TAMARA: Give us an example.

LUKA: Well, for example, you smoke a joint—

TAMARA: Okay.

LUKA: It changes the way you behave and the way you react.

TAMARA: Okay so what are you going to do? Are you going to kill somebody? Are you going to kill yourself? Are you going to steal?

LUKA: Well, it is hard to predict, and this is the biggest danger.

TAMARA: Okay, can you define paternalism?

LUKA: Well, go ahead.

TAMARA: Okay. Okay, do you think that the state should define ethical standards and moral values?

LUKA: Well, we say the state should make laws.

TAMARA: But should the state dictate the morals of the society?

LUKA: No.

TAMARA: No, the state should not decide, for example, what books and movies are available?

LUKA: The state has the right to censor material that endangers human rights.

TAMARA: Okay, but your answer is that the state has no right to decide what is moral for the individual in the society?

LUKA: It has to decide what is legal and what is illegal.

TAMARA: But not what is moral?

LUKA: Well, usually things that are legal are also moral.

TAMARA: Okay, but does the state have the right to decide what is moral for an individual.

LUKA: Yes, in some cases.

TAMARA: In some cases. Okay. Thank you.

SECOND AFFIRMATIVE (EMA)

EMA: Hello. Now, what the negative side has told us is that soft drugs should not be legalized because they are harmful to the individual and the community. Negative says soft drugs cause significant physical and psychological damage. Usage can result in brain, lung, and heart disorders and even impotence. Now, we might even agree that all these things are possible. But they are possible only when soft drugs are abused, just as they can result from the abuse of other substances, such as alcohol, cigarettes, or greasy foods.

This side of the house is advocating legalization, which is not the same thing as advocating unrestricted use, and this brings me to the psychological aspect. Now, the negative team said that soft drugs affect the mood and behavior of a person using them. We would really like to hear some evidence as to how many people are affected. How severe are these mood swings, do they really result in extreme violence?

Regarding harm to the community, negative says the use of soft drugs is escapism. But escapism is a normal thing. We all have a need to escape from reality from time to time, *says at first that the state should not dictate the morals of society, but later admits that they do, in some unspecified cases. Once again, Luka seems intent on avoiding the question. He would have done better to ask for a clarification of what Tamara meant by "moral," as distinct from "legal."*

In this exchange, Tamara has tried to win some concessions that will help the affirmative case, and she has asked for clarifications and specifications about the negative case. She has not gained much for the team tactically, however. Fundamentally, she has allowed Luka to reassert some of the basic tenets of the negative case: that the state is justified in restricting substances that are harmful to individuals, and that soft drugs are harmful. In other words, the negative position has not been changed significantly by this exchange. Luka, for his part, could have been more direct. His instinct, in the face of some very aggressive questioning, was to answer questions obliquely.

COMMENTARY ON THE AFFIRMATIVE REBUTTAL AND REFUTATION

In Chapter Ten, we discussed the dual nature of this speech. In the first place, the affirmative speaker must refute the negative case, which she has now heard in full. Secondly, she must rebut the attacks that the negative team has made upon the affirmative case.

Ema begins by refuting the negative case. She does a good job of isolating one of the key themes of the negative case: that soft drugs have harmful effects. Her challenge is a tactical mistake, however: she says that the affirmative side might agree to this argument, and invites the negative team to provide evidence. Luka had actually promised that evidence would be provided in the second negative speech; his teammate Katarina will shortly deliver on that promise. This tactic—daring the opposition to provide evidence—can only be successful if there is no evidence to provide. What is more, the affirmative team itself is open to the same charge. They have asserted that soft drugs are no more harmful than alcohol and cigarettes, but have offered no evidence.

and we just have to turn on the television to do so. Of course, negative says, we need to have responsible citizens and we will not have responsible citizens if we allow them to use soft drugs. I will deal with this part of their argument later. Negative also says we are advocating the legalization of soft drugs for egotistical reasons because drug use benefits neither the community nor to the individual. Now, I would say completely the opposite. Because the greatest benefit for the individual and for society as a whole derives from protecting the individual's right to free choice.

Now, we need to be responsible. This is what the negative side said, and we agree, but we cannot be responsible if we don't have the opportunity to be responsible. Now, if we don't have the chance to be responsible, that means we don't really have the ability to choose, because someone has already made decisions for us. Big Brother has decided that drug use is not good, and he may also decide that this book is not good, or that that picture is not good, and that people who say certain things should not be allowed to speak in public.

We believe that the most basic principles of democracy are that everyone is equal and that everyone has a say in everything. As long as you are not endangering others, you have the right to say what you wish, and others have the right to listen and decide for themselves whether they are going to do what you advocate or choose another option. This is our first argument: we need to exercise our right to free choice and we must not to put any limitations on it.

I will now address the pragmatic benefits of legalizing soft drugs, both for the individual and for the community. For the individual, there are three benefits: quality control, price control, and minimization of the forbidden fruit effect. Quality control basically means that, as we see in the Netherlands, the state will enforce certain standards in drugs sold. The consumer will be certain that drugs he or she purchases are the least harmful they can be. Negative asks what we mean by "not harmful enough." In an article in the journal *The Humanist*, it is argued that the abuse of soft drugs is equally harmful as the abuse of alcohol or the abuse of cigarettes, and since these are not illegal, soft drugs should not be illegal, because anything can be abused.

Now, when we talk about price control, we mean that legalization will create a free market for drugs, so competition will cause prices to decline, which is also beneficial for the consumer. Regarding the forbidden fruit effect, which my first speaker mentioned, and which has been compared to theft, I must say this is not a fair comparison. By stealing from somebody you directly endanger him. This is not the case with the use of soft drugs. Negative said, essentially, "If you legalize theft, you will have more theft, therefore if you legalize soft drugs, you will have more soft drugs users and abuses." But this is not so as we can see from the example of the Netherlands, where the usage of soft drugs has decreased.

Now let us examine the benefits of legalization for the community. Negative accused us of being hypocritical. But we cannot deny that if drugs were legalized, the state would tax them. What we are saying is that this money can be used for the benefit of society, for different programs that often don't get enough funding. And of course we have the reallocation of resources, this means time, money, and manpower. Think of how much time, how much money, and how much manpower goes to catching the people who are connected with the soft drug scene. One-third of all prisoners in Western Europe are in prison because of drug-related crimes. Think of how much less time, less money, and how many fewer people could be dealing with these kind of things, and dealing instead with, for example, hard drugs.

Ema would have done better to reject the importance of the negative argument—whether or not it is true. That is, she could have argued that the state has no right to interfere with individuals unless they are doing harm to other people. So it doesn't matter if drugs are harmful to the user; whether they are, or whether they aren't, the state has no right to interfere.

The second strain of her refutation is not really effective, and depends on twisting the meaning of words used by the negative team. The negative team argued that drug users drop out of society and do not fulfill their social obligations; they had called this escapism. Here, Ema calls escapism normal, and equates it with watching television. She would have done better to attack the negative team for exaggeration: drug users do not necessarily drop out of society. Her second quibble is over the word "responsible." The negative team had used this to mean the active performance of duties to society. Ema takes it to mean someone who has free choice, and reiterates the affirmative position. Again, she has not really refuted the affirmative argument—although she might well have argued that citizens do not have positive obligations towards society, and that their only responsibility is to leave other people alone.

Ema's refutation flows directly into her rebuttal. To a great degree, her rebuttal consists of repeating the terms of the affirmative argument. In his refutation, Luka had argued that the state had a right to limit free choice, but she does not address this directly in her rebuttal. She might have conceded that the state does have the right to limit free choice in certain circumstances—but that drug use, since it is personal, is not under the state's control. Although she alludes to the "endangerment of others" as a qualifying factor, she concludes the first part of her rebuttal by insisting that free choice should not be limited in any way.

Her rebuttal then moves to a consideration of the second argument offered in the original case. Ema explains the concepts of "price control and quality control" more fully than before, but she does not directly address the negative argument that it makes no sense to reduce the price of something bad, or ensure the quality of something harmful. What does emerge in her argument, however, is an explicit statement of something that Martina had mentioned briefly, in her discussion of the criterion, in the constructive speech. Here, Ema offers an argument by analogy: soft drugs are like cigarettes and alcohol, and are harmful only if they are abused; since cigarettes and alcohol are legal, then soft drugs should also be legal. This, actually, is a major argument, and should have been made explicitly in the constructive speech. It contains a key concept: that soft drugs are not harmful enough to warrant restriction. But, as we noted earlier, "harmful enough" was not explained in the constructive speech, and when Martina was asked about it explicitly in cross-examination, she replied that a full answer would be coming later.

Ema does address one part of the refutation explicitly: she rejects the argument from analogy, that drug use is like theft, and will increase if legalized. In response, she offers an argument from example—which is not powerful, because she has only one example of a country where drug use declined after legalization. She also addresses the negative charge that it would be hypocritical for the state to make money from something harmful; instead of addressing the moral argument, however, she focuses on the benefits that would come from having more money. She closes by restating one of the affirmative arguments, which has not been addressed by the negative team.

Now we come to demystification and destigmatization. This basically means that we can talk about drug use more freely, which is one of the main things in a democratic society— to be able to talk about everything. If we spoke about drug use more openly, then the people who use drugs wouldn't be regarded as bad. There is a positive side to marijuana use. It can be used as a cure for arthritis or glaucoma, and most people don't really know that, and that is because there is a stigma connected to marijuana use in general. There is a negative aura, and whoever uses marijuana is seen as bad. Now, there is also the effect legalization would have on the black market, which the first speaker mentioned. For all these reasons we beg you to vote for the affirmative, thank you.

CROSS-EXAMINATION OF THE SECOND (EMA) BY FIRST NEGATIVE (LUKA)

LUKA: Hello, I would like to ask you a few questions.

EMA: Go ahead.

LUKA: Okay, do you have the right, for example, to bang your head against the wall, if you want to?

EMA: Yes.

LUKA: And, so you have the right to hurt yourself?

EMA: Yes.

LUKA: Okay, does the state have the right to protect you, generally?

EMA: Yeah, generally, yes.

LUKA: Okay, does your right to harm yourself, preclude the state's right to try to protect you?

EMA: I wouldn't say preclude, but I would say my right is more important.

LUKA: Okay, what is the benefit to society if it allows individuals hurt themselves, and does not protect them?

EMA: You cannot look at it like that. You have to look at the benefit of letting individuals decide.

LUKA: To do the harm?

EMA: Both the harm and the good.

LUKA: Okay, you said everything can be abused.

EMA: Yes.

LUKA: If we have one thing that is wrong, does that mean we should accept another wrong?

EMA: No.

LUKA: So, are you suggesting we need one wrong more, or one wrong less?

EMA: We have the wrong and the wrong, you know, we have them both.

LUKA: Okay, does selling slaves bring money?

EMA: It would.

LUKA: Okay, if slavery were legal, would it bring revenue to the state?

EMA: If there were state slaves, yes.

LUKA: Okay, is it good just because it is profitable?

EMA: No.

LUKA: Okay, you said something about glaucoma. Are soft drugs currently available for medical purposes?

EMA: Yes, in some places in California.

LUKA: Really? Do horror movies cause impotence?

EMA: I really don't know.

LUKA: Okay, do fatty foods impair male development during puberty?

EMA: They might.

LUKA: Okay, can you get lung cancer by looking at a picture, or reading a book?

EMA: No, but if you are reading a book on a public bench in a park, you know, in very smoggy town, you could get lung cancer.

In sum, there are many missed opportunities in this speech, with regard to both refutation and rebuttal. Ema would also have done well to summarize the points of difference between the two sides. At this point in the debate, it becomes possible to see what it will take to win the argument. The affirmative team can win if they can establish that drugs are not as harmful as negative suggests, and that people who use drugs do not stop being useful and responsible citizens.

COMMENTARY ON THE SECOND NEGATIVE CROSS-EXAMINATION

Luka begins his questioning with an unusual tactic: he asks a question that lets Ema, on the affirmative side, assert that she has a right to harm herself. He follows by asking if the state has a right to protect individuals. Ema admits that it does, although it would be in her best interests to say that the state has a right to protect individuals only when someone else is injuring them. Having established that there are two such rights, Luka asks which is greater. Ema, naturally, responds that the right to harm oneself is more important. Tactically, Luka has pursued a dead end. He had no reason to believe that Ema would say anything else.

Luka then tries to tie Ema's statement back to the affirmative criterion: he asks how there can be a benefit to the community if individuals choose to harm themselves. Ema, wisely, deflects the question, by answering that choosing is itself a benefit. Luka, however, uses his next question to draw out the implication of her position: that it is somehow a benefit to choose to do harm.

The affirmative team has argued in its constructive speech that the legalization of drugs will increase tax revenue for the state. As we noted earlier, that argument was weak, and Luka exploits that weakness by introducing another example of a potentially lucrative activity; viz., slavery. Here, his questioning is successful: Ema must admit that slavery would not be considered good just because it would produce tax revenues. The corollary is that tax revenue cannot, by itself, make the legalization of drugs a good thing.

In the next section of the exchange, Luka asks a series of rhetorical questions that will allow his team to reiterate that drug use has greater harmful effects than other activities that might be banned. He follows that with a question aimed at the slippery slope conjured up in the affirmative constructive, that banning drugs leads to censorship and other restrictions on liberty. Ema says she doesn't know if there is censorship in the United States—because it would be a ruinous admission if she said that there is not.

LUKA: Okay. And you said something about the censorship of books.

EMA: Yes.

LUKA: Is there, in the United States, where soft drugs are banned, is there censorship of books?

EMA: In the United States?

LUKA: Yes.

EMA: I wouldn't know.

LUKA: Okay, do people act rationally after they have taken soft drugs?

EMA: They don't act as rationally as when they have not taken them.

LUKA: So, they act less rationally?

EMA: Yes.

LUKA: So you want to recognize people as rational beings, but then allow them to take actions that make them less rational?

EMA: From time to time everyone is less rational.

LUKA: Okay, so can you say that people will smoke only one joint if soft drugs are legalized?

EMA: Maybe some will smoke two or three. Some won't smoke any, they may decide they prefer ice cream.

LUKA: Okay, for example, a one-year-old baby.

EMA: When, I'm a baby?

LUKA: No, a one-year-old baby. . .

EMA: A one-year-old baby, okay.

LUKA: . . .held by a parent.

EMA: Okay.

LUKA: And the parent gets high from soft drugs. Is there a possibility that the parent will throw the baby against a wall or drop it, or something like that?

EMA: A parent who is neglecting his duties in this way is, I'm afraid, not fit to be a parent, regardless of whether soft drugs are legal.

LUKA: But doesn't soft drug use lead to neglect?

EMA: If you harm your child, you are not a good parent, regardless of whether drugs are legal.

LUKA: Okay, thank you very much.

EMA: Thank you.

SECOND NEGATIVE (KATARINA)

KATARINA: Good day to everyone present. The affirmative team made a distinction between the use and abuse of soft drugs. I would like to show you that there is no such thing as simply using drugs. There is only drug abuse. When you drink a glass of wine at dinner, you drink it because you like the taste of wine. When you drink three liters of wine a day, you don't drink it because you like the taste, you drink it to get drunk. When you smoke one joint, you don't smoke it because you like the taste of it. You smoke it to get high. For that reason, any use of soft drugs is abuse, never use.

Our first argument is that soft drugs are harmful to the individual. Here are some facts taken from Doctor Zuckerman's book *Use and Drugs*. Drug use affects the brain, causes panic and anxiety, and affects short-term memory. Marijuana affects the lungs, it has 50 percent more chemical substances than cigarettes. Of course you can get lung cancer because of your genetic structure, or because you are sitting outside on a bench in a polluted area. The state can't influence all of those cases, but the state can and must stop you from hurting yourself by smoking marijuana. Marijuana also increases the heart rate, has a negative impact on the reproductive systems of both males and females.It can cause miscarriages and lowers male testosterone levels. It negatively affects motor abilities and the immune system.

Briefly, Luka explores one of the paradoxes of the affirmative position, which is that the rational person they have evoked as the ideal citizen should be free to use a drug that would make him less rational. Luka closes by constructing a hypothetical situation, in which parents abuse a child because of drug use. He is attempting to establish that another person, the child, would be harmed because of drug use—which would undermine the affirmative argument that drug use harms no one but the user. Ema tries to avoid the implication of the scenario, by trying to make child neglect and drug use separate issues.

In sum, Luka's questioning is successful in that it leads, in one case, to an admission that damages the affirmative case (tax revenues do not make an action good). In two other cases, Ema avoids making damaging admissions, but only by claiming ignorance (of the existence of censorship in the United States) and by interpreting a scenario in her own way (when she suggests that parents who abuse children would do so even if they didn't take drugs). She has also accepted the recurring negative argument that drugs are harmful, which does not help the affirmative case.

COMMENTARY ON THE SECOND NEGATIVE SPEECH

As we noted in Chapter Eleven, the negative speaker has many tasks in this section of the debate. For one thing, she must continue to refute the affirmative case—and highlight for the audience which parts of the first refutation have not been rebutted by the affirmative. Unanswered challenges must be repeated and reinforced. The answered challenges, however, do not need to get dropped. Negative can show how the affirmative rebuttal has been inadequate. And, of course, the negative speaker must defend the negative case against the refutations made by affirmative in their last speech.

Katarina begins by attacking the affirmative argument that emerged in their last speech. Affirmative argued that soft drugs are harmful only if abused. The implication is that there is a safe and acceptable level of drug use. Katarina refutes this argument by emphasizing the psychoactive nature of soft drugs: the effect of drugs, she argues, is immediate and inevitable in a way that the effect of alcohol is not. Moreover, drugs are used only to achieve that psychoactive effect.

She then switches to rebuttal. Ema, the negative speaker, had challenged the negative team's assertion that drugs are harmful, and had invited them to provide evidence. Katarina now does so, by citing a source for some of the bad effects previously

Our second argument was that soft drugs are harmful to society. In cross-examination we heard that soft drugs make people less rational. When people are less rational, then they cannot function in society and we don't have healthy community. Legalizing marijuana would increase the number of abusers, and here is one example of how. During Prohibition in America alcohol was banned. When Prohibition ended, alcohol use and abuse increased. If we legalize marijuana, the number of users would increase. And according to *Newsweek Magazine*, the number of drug abusers in the Czech Republic increased after drug laws were liberalized there.

Affirmative's first argument is the right to freedom of choice. They say soft drugs are not harmful enough to merit restriction. How harmful do they have to be? Do dozens of people have to die before we see how harmful they are? We've seen from the facts presented here that soft drugs are indeed harmful enough to merit state restriction. In the case of something as harmful as soft drugs, the state has the right to intervene.

Affirmative's second argument concerns pragmatic benefits. The state must not earn extra money by harming its citizens. This was shown using the example of slavery. We can't legalize something merely because it is profitable. Slavery wasn't good, but it was profitable. Legalizing marijuana isn't good. It would profitable, but we can find money for the state budget in other ways.

I would like to say again that using soft drugs makes people less rational. We don't want less rational people driving cars or caring for infants. We don't want a society where people smoke marijuana at work. In America in the 1960s employers began testing the alcohol level in their employees' blood. Those tests led to less alcohol use on the job. This shows that laws affects they way we think, feel, and behave. If we legalize marijuana, then as a society we are saying: "Hey, it's good, you can use it." It's not good, as we have seen. We don't want people to have to die to see how dangerous it is. We know that it is dangerous enough to merit state intervention. Thank you.

CROSS-EXAMINATION OF THE SECOND (KATARINA) BY THE FIRST AFFIRMATIVE (MARTINA)

MARTINA: Hi, I have several questions for you.

KATARINA: Okay.

MARTINA: Tell me, does greasy food make your cholesterol higher?

KATARINA: Yes, in some cases.

MARTINA: Okay, can high cholesterol lead to a heart attack?

KATARINA: It is one thing that can lead to a heart attack, but just one of many.

MARTINA: Okay, have you ever heard of anyone dying from a heart attack?

KATARINA: Yes.

MARTINA: You have.

KATARINA: I have.

MARTINA: Have you ever heard of anybody dying from using soft drugs?

KATARINA Well, not exactly, I haven't heard of anyone who died, but the problem is that we don't

MARTINA: know—But, you haven't heard of anybody dying from using soft drugs, from smoking one joint of marijuana?

KATARINA: No, I have heard of people dying because after marijuana they started using harder drugs or committed a crime.

MARTINA: So, you have never heard of anybody dying from smoking one joint?

KATARINA: No.

mentioned. Ema has also challenged the negative argument that drug users are less responsible; now, Katarina exploits the admission, made in cross-examination, that drug users are less rational—the corollary being that they are therefore less responsible. In this context, Katarina refutes the forbidden fruit argument of the affirmative. Her evidence shows the removal of restrictions results in an increase in usage, not a decrease, as affirmative has argued.

Katarina finishes with more direct attacks on the affirmative case. She probes the vagueness of the affirmative argument that soft drugs are not harmful enough to be restricted. Affirmative has not provided a standard for judging when they are harmful enough. She moves on to exploit the admission made by Ema in cross-examination: that pragmatic benefits do not in themselves make an action good; this effectively refutes one of the original arguments of the affirmative case. She closes by reasserting negative's theme, that soft drugs cause enough damage to society to warrant restriction.

COMMENTARY ON THE SECOND AFFIRMATIVE CROSS-EXAMINATION

Martina opens with a line of questioning that is intended to establish that there are legal substances that can have harmful effects, and can even lead to death; the implication is that, according to the logic of the negative team, such substances should be banned. She then repeats a question made by her teammate Tamara, asking Katarina if she knows of anyone who died from using soft drugs. It is surprising that the question is repeated, since Luka had replied that drug use had led to death, but Katarina is less assertive. Martina follows up on this admission by asking questions that suggest that soft drugs, when used sparingly, have no harmful effects; she wants Katarina to say something that will damage the negative case. After all, the negative team has argued that drugs should be banned because they are harmful, and it will undermine their case if Katarina admits that that is not necessarily true. Martina poses her questions by going to extremes, however: it may be true that no one ever "died from smoking one joint of marijuana," but it does not follow, however, that marijuana is not harmful (see Chapter Six).

MARTINA: Okay, thank you. Tell me, can a person get drunk from drinking two glasses of wine?
KATARINA: In most cases, no, but if a person can't deal with—
MARTINA: But, there is a possibility?
KATARINA: There is a possibility, a small possibility of a person—
MARTINA: Tell me, have you ever dreamt about becoming a prostitute?
KATARINA: No.
MARTINA: You haven't?
KATARINA: No.
MARTINA: If prostitution were legalized, would you like to become a prostitute?
KATARINA: I'm not sure. I don't think so, but I'm not sure since I'm not in that situation.
MARTINA: But, you are not sure?
KATARINA: No.
MARTINA: Okay. Tell me, is alcohol legal?
KATARINA: Yes.
MARTINA: It is. Is it legal to drive a car with a blood alcohol level of more than .05 percent?
KATARINA: It's not legal, but people do it.
MARTINA: So, some things that are legal can be restricted. Is that right?
KATARINA: Yes.
MARTINA: Okay, thanks. One more question. Tell me, what does it mean to get high?
KATARINA: To jump into a different world, or—
MARTINA: To jump into a different world, okay. Can you jump into a different world from one puff of marijuana? One puff?
KATARINA: It depends on the person, yes if a person—
MARTINA: You can, from one puff, jump into another world?
KATARINA: I think I told you before, the problem with marijuana is that we don't know all the consequences of smoking it. One puff, one joint, or two, these can have different effects on different people. So, yes, it is possible to get high from one puff.
MARTINA: Okay, is it possible that some people smoke marijuana because they like the taste or smell of marijuana?
KATARINA: People smoke marijuana—
MARTINA: Is it possible—
KATARINA: —to get high.
MARTINA: But is it possible that some people smoke just for the taste and smell?
KATARINA: But whether you like it or not, you get high. So, in the end it is the same thing.
MARTINA: Okay, thanks.

THIRD AFFIRMATIVE SPEECH (TAMARA)

TAMARA: As the last speaker of the affirmative team, I would like to sum up a few of the most important points made in this debate. Most important, I would like to say that we have seen that the major policy of the negative team is paternalism. Paternalism is when a state treats citizens as if they are not responsible. Paternalism is the policy of the government controlling people by providing them with what they need, but giving them no responsibility, no freedom of choice.

The second thing we have been arguing about, which is very important, is the use and abuse of soft drugs. Now, according to the *Oxford English Dictionary*, to use something means to employ it for a purpose. Now, the purpose of marijuana is not the taste. The purpose of marijuana is to get high, therefore the use of marijuana cannot be qualified as abuse, according to the dictionary. And this is what we would legalize. We would legalize the use of marijuana to get high. Again, according to the dictionary, abuse is defined as the wrong or excessive use of something. So abuse of marijuana would be the wrong or

Martina starts one line of questioning that leads nowhere; it is unclear why she asks her opponent (offensively) if she ever dreamt of being a prostitute. She closes her questioning by trying to get Katarina to admit that there are no significant effects of infrequent drug use. She also wants her to admit the possibility that drugs are used for their taste and smell, not for their psychoactive qualities. Katarina rejects this possibility, not surprisingly. This is another instance of a tactical dead end. Martina had no reason to believe that Katarina would agree to a possibility that was not only implausible, but the exact opposite of what she had just argued in her own speech.

For the most part, Katarina upholds the negative case in this exchange. Martina's overall goal has been to establish that soft drugs are not harmful in ordinary use, but she has relied too heavily on extreme scenarios (one joint, or one puff of one joint) to make a convincing case.

COMMENTARY ON THE THIRD AFFIRMATIVE SPEECH

This is, of course, the last speech by the affirmative team. It is an opportunity for them to present their own scorecard. It is their chance to tell the judges where they have disagreed with the negative team, and why their arguments have been more successful.

To some extent, Tamara attempts to provide this summing up. She begins by offering a characterization of the negative philosophy as paternalism, a word with unfavorable connotations. This was the word she had wanted Lukas to define in cross-examination—so it's clear that this attack has been on her mind for a while. She does not describe the negative position with any precision, however. In her formulation, any restriction of rights means no choice whatsoever. She also tries to sum up later in her speech, when she claims that the negative team has not touched on the second argument of the affirmative case, about the pragmatic effects of legalization. In fact, the negative team not only touched on it, but refuted it effectively.

excessive use of marijuana. This might mean, for example taking marijuana with other substances, thus creating unknown reactions. Or it could mean smoking too much marijuana. It is exactly the same as with wine. We drink wine because it tastes good. We take marijuana to get high. We use wine, we use marijuana. But, we abuse wine to get drunk and that is bad. And we abuse marijuana when we take too much of it, and that is when all the bad things negative mentioned can happen.

Moving on to Prohibition, the problem with Prohibition was not the number of people using alcohol. The problem with Prohibition was that it criminalized alcohol and created a black market under the control of organized crime. If Prohibition really worked, it would still be in force. But it was abolished and that shows that it was flawed. Another point: Prohibition forbade alcohol consumption and punished drinkers. Legalizing soft drugs simply allows individuals to choose to use soft drugs. These are not the same. If we said we wanted to pass a law requiring marijuana use, that would be the same thing, and negative could reasonably claim that more people would use soft drugs. But we are not requiring anybody to use soft drugs. We are saying if you want to, you can. This will not cause an increase in the use of marijuana.

Moving now to the usage and non-usage of marijuana. Why do people use soft drugs? There are many motives, social and psychological. Social motives include peer pressure and rebellion. Psychological motives include curiosity and escapism. The motives for using marijuana either stay the same or disappear. In the case of curiosity, once you've tried it, you know what it is, so you're no longer curious. Regarding rebellion, people outgrow that. So, the motives either remain the same, or are lessened over time. The only additional motive that comes with legalization, according to the negative team, is that people will use drugs because it is legal. There are many things that are legal, but which people don't do. For example, guys can wear skirts if they want to, but they don't.

Regarding the harm created by soft drug use. Did you notice that negative never indicated specifically what level of marijuana intake would cause brain damage? Second, negative exaggerated a little bit in assigning such dire consequences to soft drug use. The ills they attribute to marijuana use can also result from a roller coaster ride, drinking too much, running after a bus, smoking cigarettes, or even parachuting, but all of these things are legal. We are free to choose whether we want to do these things. They say that soft drug use stops individuals from functioning well in society. But in fact, many citizens already use soft drugs and are functioning well. Society is functioning well. Finally, our argument concerning legalization's pragmatic benefits has been not mentioned at all. And I hope Iva will do this. Finally, regarding escapism, it is a normal thing, a necessity for all from time to time. And all the claims about the harm caused by soft drug use, all this harm is actually attributable to the abuse of soft drugs, which we would restrict. I would like to end by saying, please do choose life, and do choose a career, and do choose family. But before you do that, you must choose choice itself. Thank you.

THIRD NEGATIVE (IVA)

IVA: After the first cross-examination something became pretty clear to me. The affirmative team cannot distinguish between democracy and anarchy. The proof came after the third speech in which the speaker accused negative of promoting paternalism. Ladies and gentlemen, democracy and anarchy are not the same thing. Democracy does not mean everyone is allowed to do whatever he or she wants. Democracy is not unlimited freedom of choice.

She then returns to specific points made by the negative team. She tries to establish that there is a difference between the use of marijuana and the abuse of marijuana, just as there is a difference between the use and abuse of alcohol. In her own formulation, however, the proper, allowable use of marijuana is to get high, to experience a psychoactive effect. This is exactly what the negative team had contended, and it flatly contradicts the suggestion, made by her own teammate in cross-examination, that it might be possible to use marijuana to enjoy the taste. This is an unsuccessful tactic.

She then turns her attention to the matter of Prohibition in America, which was cited by the negative speaker as an instance of a law that reduced the use of alcohol. It was used as refutation of the forbidden fruit argument. She argues that legalization and Prohibition are opposites, but that is what the negative speaker had meant in the first place. She then restates the forbidden fruit argument, and asserts that legalization will reduce motivations for taking drugs. As mentioned earlier, this remains a paradoxical argument. In essence, the affirmative team ends up agreeing with the negative team that society will benefit if fewer people use drugs.

Tamara does her best work in the next section of her speech, when she accuses the negative team of exaggerating the effects of soft drug use on individuals, and the effects of drug users on society. The negative team is actually vulnerable on this point, but the affirmative team has no evidence with which to counteract them. The affirmative argument would be more powerful if they could state, with reasonable authority, that the moderate use of soft drugs does not cause health problems. Similarly, it would be good if the affirmative could show a statistical linkage between drug use and social benefits—if they could show, for example, that a country with a high rate of drug use shows a lower crime rate than a country with a lower rate of drug use. Without evidence, however, Tamara relies on the sweeping contention that society is functioning well, even though there are people who use drugs

COMMENTARY ON THE THIRD NEGATIVE SPEECH

Iva's job here is similar to Tamara's job in the previous speech. She is supposed to sum up the major points of conflict, and say why the negative team has carried those points. To some degree, Iva does so. Much of her speech is a forceful restatement of earlier points. It would have been better, however, if the summary had been more pointed, if Iva had laid out a clear list of items to be addressed. As it stands, her approach is improvisatory. Her speech would have been more powerful if she had announced, at the beginning, that she saw three major points of conflict, and then had moved through them one by one.

Iva opens with a rhetorical flourish that matches the one made by the affirmative team. Tamara had accused the negative team of paternalism. Iva counters by accusing them of

If I wanted to build a house on the main square in the city, I would not be allowed to do so. Why? Because I'd be violating certain standards and rules of society. And it is upon those rules that a democratic society is built. We cannot tolerate a society where people do whatever they want with the only proviso being that they don't harm others. The question here is not whether we are capable of making our own decisions. We are all capable of making como dooioiono. Sure, when I get into a car, I can choose whether I want to put the seatbelt on or not. But the thing is, that if I don't put it on, I'm endangering myself. And sometimes I will not put it because I'm too lazy or because I don't believe I will have an accident. That's why the state has to intervene to take care of citizens. That is what we expect from the state.

In order for the state protect us, we must grant the state certain rights. We have to give the state authority. Now, what the affirmative team hasn't proved here, is why drug legalization is so tremendously important for democracy. Why is it crucial for democracy to have drugs legalized, since in all democratic countries of the world, except for the Netherlands, drugs are currently banned, and these bans haven't lead to abuse of power? Criminalization of soft drugs hasn't lead to censorship, as affirmative suggested was possible. Drug control hasn't lead to anything negative.

The supposed distinction between drug use and abuse was also mentioned. The third speaker cited a dictionary. She said, "according to the dictionary." Well ladies and gentlemen, according to reality, there is no such thing as drug use. The speaker said that abuse means using something for the wrong reasons. Ladies and gentlemen, there are no right reasons for using marijuana. The only reason to use marijuana is to get high and that is wrong.

The second mistake made by the affirmative team was that they presumed unrealistic, ideal conditions. They presumed that all marijuana users are perfectly healthy—that they won't misuse drugs, that they won't drive while under the influence, that they won't use it while they are working, or while they are taking care of their children. But this is not so. If drugs are legalized, the state cannot prevent people from smoking at home while children are there. They cannot prevent people from using it at work. By legalizing drugs we are opening a Pandora's Box of bad consequences. We certainly won't be able to prevent people from using hard drugs, once they realize that soft drugs are not good enough anymore.

The third issue raised was the question of motivation. Whether we want to admit it or not, the fact is that laws do influence the way people think and the way people feel. Many people, especially young people, fear the law. They are not willing to risk arrest, so they don't use drugs. If we legalize drugs, that we will remove this fear. People who are currently afraid of the laws will have nothing to fear.

Moreover, laws provide standards in a society. Laws tell us what's wrong, and what's right. And if society tells us that using drugs is a normal thing, that ladies and gentlemen, cannot lead to good for the society. Let me remind you that the good of the community is our mutual criterion.

The main excuse offered by affirmative team is that there are a lot of other bad things in the world, so we might just as well legalize soft drugs. Ladies and gentlemen, that is no excuse. There are many things we can't fight, but we can and should fight soft drugs.

Affirmative's main error is that they claim to want to create responsible citizens. But they also want to make them irrational, and that is the wrong way to go about things. That is why we should not legalize soft drugs. Thank you very much.

wanting anarchy. That is an exaggeration. Fortunately, Iva explains the negative team's concept of social responsibility in more measured terms.

Iva continues by rejecting the distinction that Tamara made between use and abuse, but she misses an opportunity to point out that Tamara has agreed with one of the affirmative team's contentions: namely, that the only reason to use marijuana is to get high.

What follows is a new refutation of the affirmative case. Iva accuses the affirmative team of minimizing the effects of drug use by assuming that drugs will be used in a way that never impacts on other people. She argues that if drug use increases, it is fair to assume that there will be more instances where drug use does have an impact on other people. This is a major point for the negative team, and Iva might have highlighted it more strongly. The extent of the effect of drug use on others is one of the central differences between the two sides. The negative case depends on the assumption that society will be affected by drug use. The affirmative argument depends on the assumption that drug use affects only the user. If the negative case can refute that assumption, they should win the debate—and Iva would have done well to say so explicitly.

Iva concludes by touching on some arguments that have already been made. Once again, she refutes the forbidden fruit argument mounted by the affirmative team. She also reaffirms the negative team's argument that laws should set standards for society—this, in some ways, is a repetition of her opening argument about the rules inherent in a democracy.

Iva's arguments would be stronger if they were directed at review, rather than repetition. That is, instead of repeating the arguments against the forbidden fruit argument, she would do better to remind the judges that her teammate refuted this argument with evidence in the second negative speech, and that the affirmative team had not successfully rebutted that refutation in their response. In other words, the last speaker must resist the temptation to find new ways to make old arguments, but should instead remind judges that the arguments have already been made, and that they have been successful. The ultimate irony here is that Tamara has unwittingly conceded major points to the negative team in her last speech. Iva could have pointed out those concessions to the judges, with the corollary that the negative team must win the round.

You decide.

Appendix 2.
Introductory Debate Exercises

1. SKILLS INVENTORY

GOAL:

To demonstrate to students that they already possess many of the skills relevant to debate.

METHOD:

+ Ask students to write down at least three skills they have which they believe might help them become good debaters.

+ Students can share their answers with the class.

+ Coaches can highlight answers that reinforce the message that debate doesn't require an entirely new set of skills, but presents an opportunity to use and develop many skills and interests students already have.

GOAL:

To focus on argument construction and refutation while involving a large group of students.

METHOD:

✦ Divide the class into two halves, affirmative and negative.

✦ Then divide each group in half again, creating the first affirmatives and the second affirmatives, and the first negatives and the second negatives.

✦ Pick a topic students are familiar with.

✦ Start off by asking the first affirmatives to stand in turn and present one argument, speaking for no more than 30 seconds.

✦ The entire class should write down and number each first affirmative argument. If there are five speakers in the first affirmative group, by the time every affirmative has spoken, each student should have a list with arguments one through five, numbered as such.

✦ Before the first affirmatives start, number the first negatives and inform them that they will be responsible for refuting the corresponding affirmative argument.

✦ Once the first negatives have responded, the second group of affirmative speakers is up. Their goal is to defend one of the original affirmative arguments by attacking the negative response to that argument.

✦ Again, each person has a number, so affirmative three would be expected to defend the third affirmative argument.

✦ The second group of negative completes the process according to the same system.

3. DEBATE REPORTER

GOAL:
To involve students who are attending debate tournaments, but not yet ready to participate.

METHOD:

✦ Ask new or potential team members to attend a debate tournament. Tell them to bring a notebook and ask them to act as a **"reporter"** for the tournament.

✦ **"Reporters"** should make note of the conventions, or informal rules, of debate that they observe in order create a list of the rules of good debates.

✦ Students can try to identify five things that winning teams do best.

✦ The resulting essays or lists of rules can be included in the team's newsletter.

4. SPAR DEBATES

GOAL:

To familiarize students with the idea of making arguments, asking questions, and judging the strength of competing arguments.

METHOD:

+ List a number of common, easily debatable topics on the blackboard. Have two students come to the front of the room.

+ After a coin toss, the winning student selects the topic and the loser chooses the side.

+ Each debater receives five minutes to prepare.

+ Then a very quick debate occurs:
  > **Affirmative constructive (90 seconds),**
  > **cross-examination (60 seconds),**
  > **negative opening speech (90 seconds),**
  > **cross-examination (60 seconds),**
  > **affirmative closing (45 seconds),**
  > **negative closing (45 seconds).**

+ To keep the exercise running quickly, two students can be preparing while another two are debating.

+ The debate lasts about as long as the preparation time.

+ Following the debates the class and the instructor or coach can take the opportunity to discuss strong arguments, strategies, and goals to work toward in the future.

(Courtesy of the Emory National Debate Institute, Gordon Mitchell and the Pittsburgh Urban Discussion and Debate League.)

5. STUDENT PARLIAMENT

GOAL:

To use an expanded debate setting to allow students to consider and discuss a variety of policy proposals.

METHOD:

✦ Divide students into three or more political parties. If they wish they can name their party and create a philosophy, but it isn't necessary.

✦ Have each student create a **"bill"**
(a policy proposal, a new law, or a change to an existing law).

✦ Make a list of all of the bills from each party.

✦ Allow members of each party to look at the list of bills proposed by the other two parties. They must select at least half of those bills to oppose.

✦ Give students about ten minutes of preparation time in which to think about how they will defend their own bill how they will attack the bills that their party has decided to oppose.

✦ Once the preparation time ends, a parliamentary assembly begins.
The instructor, acting as the speaker of the house invites the consideration of each bill in turn, with some students making speeches in favor of the bill, and other students making speeches against the bill.

✦ When the speeches die out, each bill is voted up, or down.

EXERCISES IN ARGUMENT CONSTRUCTION

GOAL:

To help students understand the process of putting ideas together so that the ideas are logical, understandable, and persuasive.

METHOD:

◆ Take an organized argument, perhaps one previously prepared by an experienced debater.

◆ Divide it so that each idea and quotation appears on a separate sheet of paper.

◆ Then ask students to re-assemble the argument.

◆ The instructor can then lead a discussion on the various solutions, taking note that there may be several good ways to structure the argument, some of which may be even better than the way the argument was originally structured.

EXERCISES IN ARGUMENT CONSTRUCTION

GOAL:
To familiarize students with new evidence and promote the idea that evidence must be explained in order to make an argument sound.

METHOD:

✦ Each student is assigned one or more quotations. Instruct student to stand before the class and:

Make an argument in a single sentence

Support that argument by reading the quotation

Follow-up with a two to four sentence discussion of why quotation is relevant

✦ The instructor should encourage students to be concise, to choose words carefully, to accurately represent what the quotation is saying, and to apply the quotation in a strategic fashion.

**EXERCISES IN
THE SOCIAL ROLE
OF DEBATE**

GOAL:

To reinforce the idea that many things are debatable, even subjects on which the student already has an opinion.

METHOD:

✦ Ask students to make a list of ten possible topics for debate and to place each subject in one of three categories:

> **Subjects on which they hold a strong opinion and against which they probably could not argue effectively**
>
> **Subjects on which they have an opinion, but against which they could argue**
>
> **Subjects on which they have no real opinion**

✦ Students should try to allocate at least one topic to each category.

✦ The instructor can lead a discussion about which topics ended up in which categories and emphasize that many topics are quite debatable.

✦ Instructors can also discuss on the criteria for debatability.

EXERCISES IN THE SOCIAL ROLE OF DEBATE

GOAL:

To encourage students to draw a connection between skills learned in educational debate, and debate as it occurs outside the classroom.

METHOD:

✦ Obtain videotape of some kind of social debate. This can be a discussion among political candidates, a forum of policy experts, or a disagreement on a local talk show.

✦ After showing the video tape, the instructor can lead the class in a discussion of the debate elements that appeared in the tape.

What resolution(s) did they seem to be debating?

What contentions were offered?

Was evidence presented?

Was the reasoning offered adequate?

Were there moments of cross-examination?

**EXERCISES IN
THE SOCIAL ROLE
OF DEBATE**

GOAL:
To encourage students to think about audience analysis as an essential component in creating arguments in public fora.

METHOD:

✦ Select a situation in which students have recently made or will soon make an argument to a particular person or group. Then ask them to:

> **Think of at least three strategies for finding out information about an audience's values and attitudes**
>
> **Decide which strategies would appear credible to this audience.**
>
> **Decide how to incorporate that information into planning a message**

✦ The instructor and students can discuss ways to adapt to an audience and how this differs from simply molding one's own opinions to accommodate an audience.

(Courtesy of the Pfeiffer Critical Thinking CD-ROM)

EXERCISES IN PREPARATION AND ANALYSIS

GOAL:
To demonstrate techniques of brainstorming.

METHOD:

✦ Present the following scenario:
The largest paperclip factory in the world is for sale and you have the option to buy it. You must justify the purchase to your investors. Number your ideas as you go along.

✦ Encourage teams of students to get to work, following several rules about brainstorming:

Don't try to decide which ideas are good or bad, just write them all down

Wild or unusual ideas are acceptable

Go for quantity, try to produce as many ideas as possible

Don't be too serious, if you aren't laughing then you aren't doing it right

(Courtesy of the Pfeiffer Critical Thinking CD-ROM.)

EXERCISES IN
PREPARATION
AND ANALYSIS

GOAL:

To help students to understand the importance of complete analysis:
the relationship between issues, resolutions, definitions, and arguments.

METHOD:

✦ With a partner, select and develop 10 issues over which reasonable people
could disagree.

✦ After discussing these "resolutions," pick one or two and:

**Phrase the subject as a question about which two sides
in a debate would disagree**

Phrase it as a resolution

Define controversial words

**Identify the likely arguments to be
expected from each side, pro and con**

**EXERCISES IN
PREPARATION
AND ANALYSIS**

GOAL:

To encourage students to begin the process of thinking about where a resolution comes from, why it is important, and how it is likely to be debated.

METHOD:

✦ Using a resolution that students are likely to debate in the future, ask students to complete the following statements on paper:

> **The resolution is relevant because...**
>
> **The background of this resolution is important because...**
>
> **The resolution contains several key terms that are...**
>
> **These terms are defined as...**
>
> **This resolution contains several key issues, including...**
>
> **Affirmatives should keep in mind that...**
>
> **Negatives should keep in mind that...**

✦ After completing the statements, students can work in small groups to develop more comprehensive answers. Finally, all of the answers can be shared and discussed by the class.

EXERCISES IN PREPARATION AND ANALYSIS

GOAL:

To promote an understanding of the three general types of resolutions and to initiate a discussion on the differences in analysis that accompany each.

METHOD:

✦ Present the students with a list of about ten resolutions and ask them which ones are fact, which are value, and which are policy. You can invent your own resolutions or use the following:

> **The earth is being visited by beings from other planets (fact)**
>
> **President Clinton is an effective leader (value)**
>
> **Dogs are better than cats (value)**
>
> **People should not eat animals (policy)**
>
> **Expansion of NATO has promoted peace and stability in Europe (fact)**
>
> **The state should provide education only in its official language (policy)**
>
> **Some people are able to move objects with 'psychic energy' (fact)**
>
> **This country ought to have open borders (policy)**
>
> **Pollution is currently causing global warming (fact)**
>
> **Individual autonomy is more important than community (value)**

✦ Following the identification of resolutions, instructors can ask questions to show that different types of resolutions carry different burdens: for example, policy resolutions require the defense of some kind of action while fact and value resolutions require some kind of criterion or standard.

GOAL:

To encourage students to focus on what makes a resolution good or bad.

METHOD:

✦ Present students with a list of possible resolutions, including some recently debated resolutions. Include some that are unclear, some that contain no controversy, some that have obviously biased language, some that focus on multiple ideas, and some that focus on insignificant or uninteresting issues.

✦ Working alone or in groups, students should accept or reject each resolution and give a reason for their decision.

✦ As students present their reasons to the class, the instructor can record all of the criteria for good resolutions that get mentioned.

**EXERCISES IN
PREPARATION
AND ANALYSIS**

GOAL:
To reinforce the notion that only some terms need to be defined, and to initiate a discussion on what makes a definition good or bad.

METHOD:

✦ Using a list of recent resolutions, ask students to indicate which terms might require definition.

✦ Then ask students to brainstorm about ways to define those terms and to discuss which definitions might be better and why.

✦ As students present their choices to the class, the instructor can keep a list of the criteria for developing good definitions.

17. DICTIONARY CHALLENGE

GOAL:

To acquaint students with the use of dictionaries as a means of clarifying the debate.

METHOD:

◆ If you have access to several dictionaries, pick one resolution and challenge the students to find as many different definitions as possible.

◆ Have students present their definitions to the class and give awards for several categories: most reasonable, most unexpected but still reasonable, most distorted, most useless, and so on.

◆ The instructor may also want to stage a minidebate on definitions by having two students argue over which definition is more reasonable.

◆ The goal in such a debate would be to emphasize that students should give brief, clear reasons why their definition would lead to a better debate, and to emphasize that such a definitional dispute would never characterize an entire debate, but only a moment in a debate.

**EXERCISES IN
PREPARATION
AND ANALYSIS**

GOAL:

To teach students to read with purpose when doing research.

METHOD:

✦ Provide students with a short article (the shorter the better) on a topic which they will be debating.

✦ Move through the article, sentence by sentence, either individually or as a class, and discuss whether a particular idea, fact, or quotation would be useful for a debate.

✦ It is important for students to identify the specific claim that research materials would support, and to summarize arguments in one sentence (sometimes called a "tag").

19. SOURCE SELECTION

EXERCISES IN PREPARATION AND ANALYSIS

GOAL:
To teach students to determine quickly whether a source is going to be useful.

METHOD:

✦ Gather several books related to a debate topic.
Not all of them have to be good ones.

✦ Distribute the books and have students evaluate the book's usefulness for the topic by considering the following elements below.

The title

The table of contents

The index

The preface or introduction

One or two passages, selected at random

✦ Discuss which books might be best to use and why.

GOAL:

To practice flowing and learn about current events at the same time.

METHOD:

✦ Ask students take notes on the evening news, just as they would flow a debate.

✦ Numbering each story, the student should write down:

> **A title for the story**
> **(e.g., "U.S.A. finally pays its UN dues")**
>
> **Some salient facts about the story**
> **(e.g., $1.5 billion was owed.)**
>
> **Name of people who were quoted in the story**
> **(e.g., Madeline Albright.)**

✦ This simple exercise provides very realistic practice on a daily basis. The current events that the students learn will be useful in debates.

**EXERCISES IN
PREPARATION
AND ANALYSIS**

GOAL:

To encourage students to think about a debate after it has ended and to focus on future improvement.

METHOD:

✦ Debaters may wish to forget a debate once it ends. To avoid repeating the same mistakes over again, it is important to encourage debaters to focus on improvement while the debate is still fresh in their heads.

✦ Sitting with a coach after a round, debaters should specifically review what was said and discuss question such as:

What were the strongest arguments?

What argument presented the greatest challenge?

How could arguments be rethought to be more resistant to attack?

✦ If coaches cannot be physically present, a post-debate questionnaire can pose the same questions. Coaches can review the answers at another time.

**EXERCISES
IN FORMAT**

GOAL:
To get students to remember the format of debate by practicing with a fun
and easy topic.

METHOD:

✦ Pick a very easy topic and have two teams of students go through the motions
of giving speeches within the conventional format.

✦ In running this exercise, it is not important how long the students speak, and
it is not really important whether they make good arguments or not. What
is important is that they develop a sense of **"who speaks when."**

✦ The instructor can pause between speeches in order to talk about the goal of the
upcoming speech or cross-examination period.

EXERCISES IN FORMAT

GOAL:

To provide students with a detailed understanding of what a debate looks like.

METHOD:

✦ Have students watch a debate, either performed live by experienced debaters, or on videotape. The debate doesn't need to be perfect. In fact, it may be better if it is flawed. Students will be less intimidated and will get a chance to discuss how the debate might have been improved.

✦ While watching the debate, students should keep a written flow, as well as notes on what they liked or disliked and a list of terms and arguments that they did not understand.

✦ Afterwards, the instructor can lead a discussion on several themes:

What were the main arguments advanced in the debate?

What arguments did students disagree with most, and why?

What strategies would students have used in answering the arguments made in the debate?

What were students' favorite part of the debate, and why?

GOAL:
To encourage students to convert ideas into structured claims.

METHOD:

✦ Using a simple resolution, ask students to write down:

**A title for the contention, or claim that supports
the resolution**

**An introductory statement, a sentence or two
that explains the contention**

**Subpoint A, the first reason or way in which
the contention is true**

**Subpoint B, the second reason or way in which
the contention is true**

GOAL:

To convey to students the idea that many claims include an underlying value, or criterion, and to reinforce the idea that a criterion is a natural component of any argument.

METHOD:

+ Find some value claims (for example in advertisements or newspaper editorials) and ask students to identify the assumed value which underlies the claim and discuss how that assumed value might be expressed as a criterion.

+ For example, an advertisement that encourages us to eat a particular hamburger because it tastes better upholds the idea of taste or flavor as the most important value.

+ A criterion of **"we ought to prefer hamburgers with the best flavor"** is being offered instead of other potential criteria such as, **"We ought to prefer hamburgers with the best nutrition, or hamburgers with the lowest cost."**

**EXERCISES
IN AFFIRMATIVE
CASE
CONSTRUCTION**

GOAL:
To help students understand and remember the components of the affirmative case.

METHOD:

✦ Create signs with string that can hang around each student's neck. On each sign, write one component of the case:

Introduction

Conclusion

Definitions

Criterion

Contention I

Contention II

Contention III

✦ Hang a sign on each student. You can assign multiple students to one component or multiple components to one student in order to even up the numbers.

✦ Give students a fixed amount of time to discuss and prepare their component. Depending on how advanced they are you can do this with evidence, or without.

✦ In the end, the case gets presented in order (from introduction through conclusion) with each person delivering their component of the case while wearing their sign.

EXERCISES IN CROSS-EXAMINATION

GOAL:

To practice cross-examination and teamwork, and to understand that cross-examination is best when it focuses on a series of questions.

METHOD:

- ◆ Split the class into two groups.

- ◆ One group composes an argument for a resolution while the other group composes an argument against the resolution.

- ◆ Each side presents their argument.

- ◆ Then one group becomes the **'questioners'** while the other becomes the **'responders'**. Each group has one representative standing.

- ◆ The questioner begins cross-examination and the responder responds. At any point if the questioner or the responder can't figure out what to say next, then another member of their team can "tag-in" and take their place.

- ◆ The instructor discusses the quality and strategy of the questions.

**EXERCISES IN
CROSS-
EXAMINATION**

GOAL:

To understand that cross-examination is supposed to have a goal and to emphasize that asking a series of questions is a way of getting to that goal.

METHOD:

+ Divide the class into groups as described in exercise 27.

+ This time, however, after each team has heard the other team's argument, but before questioning begins, each team writes a **"secret goal"** on paper. The secret goal is a realistic but challenging objective for cross-examination, e.g., **"I want them to admit that their idea is risky because it has never been tried."**

+ Questioning begins, it can be tag-team, or with one selected questioner and respondent.

+ Questioning ends when the questioner either announces that the goal has been reached or realizes that the questioning will be fruitless.

**EXERCISE
IN NEGATIVE
CASE
CONSTRUCTION**

GOAL:
To teach students how to negate a resolution.

METHOD:

✦ Using a resolution that students are likely to debate in the future, ask them complete the following statements on paper:

The affirmative is likely to say that...

These arguments are insufficient because...

The negative philosophy is....

✦ After completing the statements, students can be paired or can work in small groups to develop more comprehensive answers.

✦ Finally, all of the answers can be shared or discussed by the class.

**EXERCISES
IN REFUTATION
AND REBUTTAL**

GOAL:

To help student learn how to think quickly and to understand refutation.

METHOD:

✦ Students stand in a circle, the instructor throws a ball to one student.

✦ The person who catches the ball makes an argument (you can limit the subject, or leave it open) and throws the ball to another person.

✦ The person who catches the ball must either refute the argument or extend it by providing a new reason to support it.

✦ The game continues.

✦ If a player is uncertain how to answer, or if you have stayed too long on one issue, then you can make new arguments on a different issue.

**EXERCISES
IN REFUTATION
AND REBUTTAL**

GOAL:

To emphasize skills in refutation, as well as rebuttal.

METHOD:

✦ Ask each student to write on the top of a piece of paper one argument that they would be willing to defend.

✦ Pass the papers around the room so that each student has a chance to list one reason against each argument thus presented. This part of the exercise should proceed at quick pace.

✦ When each paper is returned to its original author, give students ten minutes to prepare responses to the arguments which have been made against their original proposition.

✦ Encourage students to group similar objections together and answer them at once.

✦ Finally, ask each student to stand and orally refute as many arguments against their position as possible in five minutes.

(Courtesy of the Pfeiffer Critical Thinking CD-ROM.)

**EXERCISES
IN REFUTATION
AND REBUTTAL**

GOAL:
To build confidence in public speaking.

METHOD:

✦ Pick a topic that is familiar to all students.

✦ Assign each student a number.

✦ Ask student number one to give a speech on the selected topic.

✦ Instruct the other students to be alert for three errors:

**Repetition
(beyond that required for clarity)**

**Assertion
(making a statement without any evident
attempt to support it)**

**Deviation
(straying from the topic)**

✦ When the first speaker errs, the next student takes up the argument.

✦ The speech continues until it becomes impossible to say anything
without repeating, asserting, or deviating.

**EXERCISES
IN REFUTATION
AND REBUTTAL**

GOAL:

To understand that there is a sequence to good refutation.

METHOD:

✦ Divide the class into four-person groups.

✦ Present an argument to the groups.

✦ Each group must develop a refutation. To emphasize the steps, the first person states the argument that will be refuted, the second person states the claim that will be used to refute that argument, the third person supports that claim, and the fourth person states the impact, or shows why the refutation is important.

**EXERCISES
IN CONCLUDING
ARGUMENTS**

GOAL:

To encourage students to think about strategic choices and means of comparing arguments in the final rebuttal.

METHOD:

✦ Present students with the following scenario, or a similar one of the instructor's own invention: *You are the third speaker for the negative team, and you are late for the debate. You arrive to find that you are the next speaker. The resolution is* **"Resolved: television reduces the quality of modern life."** *Your team opposes this resolution. Affirmative has argued that television's violent content (especially news broadcasts) encourages violence in society. Your team responded that not all television content is violent, and that news is a vital part of a democratic society. Your team challenged the affirmative team to present evidence that people mimic the news. Affirmative did not respond to the point of news being vital, but presented an example of a person copying a violent act seen on the news. The affirmative team also argued—most emphatically to the judges in their last speech—that television lacks serious educational content. Your team did not address this issue. They also argued that politicians use television to lie to the public. They presented no examples, but simply said it happens all the time. Your team responded by saying that television also allows the media to uncover the lies, but similarly presented no examples. Your team argued that modern means "in the present generation." Affirmative argued that it means "in the present century." Affirmative presented statistics showing that crime and violence have risen at the same time that television has become more prevalent in society. Your team countered that it did not follow that crime and violence increased because of television. Your team's first argument was that television informs society, current events programming, weather, public service announcements were cited. Affirmative responded that the information was usually violent, incorrect, or purposefully misleading. Your team's second argument was that entertainment is a vital social need, and that television entertains. This was supported with a quotation from a psychologist saying that television helps people relax and reduces stress. Affirmative responded that they didn't find television entertaining—they said they preferred books.*

✦ Ask and discuss the following questions:

What are the issues, how many are there?

Which issues are important, which unimportant?

How should we address an issue that was dropped?

How should we handle an issue that the other side might be winning?

How do we tell the judge whose reasoning, evidence, or examples are better?

How do we put all of this together into a reason to vote for one side or the other?

EXERCISES IN CONCLUDING ARGUMENTS

GOAL:

To demonstrate that arguments can always be improved.

METHOD:

- ✦ This exercise works best in a one-on-one setting with a coach and a student.

- ✦ Ask the student to deliver the final speech from a debate in which the student participated, or which he observed and flowed.

- ✦ Ask the student to tear off the final column of the flow and to attach blank column.

- ✦ Instruct the student to deliver the final speech again, up to three times, each time using the blank column of his flow as a tool to improve the argument incrementally.

GOAL:

To demonstrate that the spoken word differs from the written word.

METHOD:

✦ Select one or two paragraphs from a book or magazine.

✦ Ask students to rewrite the passage for a speech, incorporating elements of oral style.

✦ Students should be instructed to:

Use the active voice

Use familiar and concrete rather than formal and abstract language

Use personal pronouns

Use sentences with few clauses and modifying phrases

Use more repetition

Compare the written and spoken versions and discuss what is easier to read and what is easier to listen to.

EXERCISES IN STYLE AND DELIVERY

GOAL:
To help students understand the importance of language in determining the overall tone and effectiveness of communication.

METHOD:

✦ Find a short passage of text that is either positive or neutral toward a particular subject.

✦ Ask students to rewrite the passage by changing the word choices but maintaining the overall direction of the message. Their goal is to make the message unclear, or to make the message seem to support the opposite side, simply by replacing selected words.

✦ For example, consider the following passage:

> **"Turkey lovers far and wide insist upon the freshest possible bird."**

This could be subversively rewritten to read:

> **Those scattered people who enjoy ingesting the dead flesh of a Turkey want to consume that carcass as soon after it is killed as possible.**

The general statement is the same, but the word choice makes it a different message altogether.

**EXERCISES IN
STYLE AND
DELIVERY**

GOAL:
To help students develop and organize thoughts quickly and clearly.

METHOD:

✦ Prepare a number of possible topics for debate.

✦ Randomly assign topics to students.

✦ Allow each student two to five minutes to prepare before delivering a speech of five to seven minutes on the assigned topic.

✦ The point is not to produce high quality content but to hone students' ability to think quickly, to divide a topic into two or more main points, and to apply present knowledge to the topic at hand.

EXERCISES IN STYLE AND DELIVERY

GOAL:

To relax in preparation for public speaking.

METHOD:

✦ There are several ways to relax the vocal chords and the body in preparation for public speaking:

Make horse noises by forcing air between your closed lips. This loosens the muscles around the mouth.

Speed-drills: read aloud at different speeds to get the eyes and the tongue accustomed to working together.

Stretch your face muscles by trying to get your mouth, nose, and eyebrows as close together as possible, then as far apart as possible.

Tension in any part of the body can cause stumbling and shaking, any body stretching is good preparation for public speaking, in particular neck-rolls, in which the head is brought toward one shoulder, then to the front, then to the other shoulder.

GOAL:
To promote clear speech.

METHOD:

✦ Every language has its **"tongue-twisters."** The following are some of the favorites in English:

> **Toy boat**
>
> **Red leather, yellow leather**
>
> **Rubber baby buggy bumpers**
>
> **The lips, the tongue, and the teeth**

Repeating one of these phrases over and over again, with increasing speed and with an attempt to keep every sound separate and correct, can improve articulation.

✦ Longer drills also exist.

For example, this British one: *"What a 'to do' to die today at a minute or two to two.A thing distinctly hard to say, and harder still to do is to beat a tattoo at twenty to two with a rat-tat-tat-tat-tat-tat-too at two, and the dragon will come when he hears the drum, at a minute or two to two today, at a minute or two to two."*

Don't ask what it means, just say it fast!

**EXERCISES IN
STYLE AND
DELIVERY**

GOAL:

To help students give particular words special emphasis.

METHOD:

✦ Encourage students to read aloud selections from poetry that require special emphasis and feeling.

✦ Encourage students to vary pitch, rate, and inflection in order to convey the meaning and importance of various phrases. Also ask students to underline key words and phrases which should receive special stress.

✦ In addition to using poetry, you can ask students to read aloud their own or someone else's speeches. Ask them to underline key words in the text and to indicate where a pause might be effective.

**EXERCISES IN
DEVELOPING A
DEBATE CLUB**

GOAL:

To encourage students to focus on the goal of the team.

METHOD:

✦ Working individually, in groups, or all together, ask students to create a mission statement for the team.

✦ The instructor can use portions of the different documents produced by students to facilitate the creation of a final draft.

> **A mission statement is a short paragraph, three to five sentences, which identifies the team's objective.**

✦ Once they've completed the statement, ask students to compare it with the team's actual activities by posing several questions.

> **Is the mission statement complete?**
>
> **Does it account for all of our activities?**
>
> **Does it match our actual objectives?**
>
> **Are we currently living up to the statement?**

✦ A mission statement is a way of promoting a discussion that focuses a team's activities and helps determine what the team ought to do. It should address issues such as:

> **To what extent are our goals competitive, educational, or both?**
>
> **To what extent do we try to reach other audiences?**
>
> **To what extent are we broadening our own base and expanding our membership?**

**EXERCISES IN
DEVELOPING A
DEBATE CLUB**

GOAL:
To encourage students to develop their own norms and practices for the operation of the team.

METHOD:

✦ As in the exercise number 42, students can work individually, in groups, or all together to create an identity for the team.

✦ This time, instead of creating a mission statement, ask them to compose a constitution to guide the operation and the leadership of the team.

✦ The instructor can use portions of the different documents produced to facilitate the creation of a final draft. The constitution should address several issues:

What is the leadership of the team?

How is the leadership selected and replaced?

How does the team record its activities and decisions?

How does the team get and spend money?

How does the team change its own policies, including the constitution?

GOAL:

To provide students with a fun way to practice, to get to know one another, and perhaps to raise a small amount of money.

METHOD:

✦ A talk-a-thon based on the word **"marathon"** simply means talking for a very long period of time.

　✦ For debate teams, it usually means talking for a full 24 hours.

　✦ Pick a day and a location, and for 24 hours straight, make sure someone from the team is giving a speech. Students may debate, deliver impromptu speeches, interpret literature, or, in the middle of the night when everyone is too tired to think, simply read aloud from a handy book.

　✦ If fundraising is a part the goal, students can ask sponsors to pledge a certain amount of money for every hour the team talks.

　✦ For students, this is a fun activity: a round-the-clock party with opportunities for socializing and speechmaking.

　✦ For instructors, well, it is a unique opportunity.

EXERCISES IN LOGIC AND REASONING

GOAL:

To encourage students to recognize the various parts of an argument (claim, data, and warrant) and to use them in evaluating arguments.

METHOD:

◆ Present students with arguments that you have created or drawn from existing sources.

◆ Ask them to identify the claim, data and warrant.

For example, if you presented the argument *the lesson today was very difficult, so I'm sure we learned a lot* students could identify the claim as *we learned a lot*, and the data as *the lesson today was very difficult*. So, the implied warrant is *difficulty causes us to learn*.

The usefulness of performing this kind of analysis is to identify the potential weaknesses of an argument, often contained in the warrant. For example, is the level of difficulty really enough for us to conclude that a lesson was educational? Analysis is the first step of criticism.

**EXERCISES IN
DEVELOPING THE
DEBATE CLUB**

GOAL:
To help students understand and apply the definition of an argument.

METHOD:

✦ Discuss what does and does not constitute an argument.

✦ Then present students with a list of statements and ask them to identify the argument as well as the statements that are not arguments. Below is a list of statements, those which meet the definition of an argument as a claim with a reason are marked with a star:

> **People should ride bicycles more, because air pollution is a problem in the city. ***
>
> **Survival is the most important and most highly respected human value.**
>
> **Our awareness of environmental problems is increasing. Already we have reduced the emission of chemicals that destroy the ozone and have banned many pesticides. ***
>
> **My opponent argues that acid rain is destroying the environment, but that is an inaccurate, incomplete and irrelevant argument.**
>
> **Species loss is at a crisis level. Harvard Biologist Edward Wilson estimates that nearly 140 species are lost every day. ***
>
> **The most important thing we can do is to protect the environment. Please, take any action you can.**
>
> **Since all pollution laws have economic consequences, we need to look at this law's effect on the economy. ***
>
> **When a species loses its natural habitat, it is nearly impossible to prevent it from going extinct. There are only a few thousand Giant Panda, for instance, now that their habitat is taken over by development. ***
>
> **How can we wait, even a single day, to take action to protect the environment?**
>
> **The move to a more environmentally conscious society will require big changes. The industrial revolution brought changes in government, family, and the economy. In the same way, the move to an ecological society will require fundamental changes. ***
>
> **Some argue that global warming will destroy the world, but they fail to prove this as they present no evidence that global warming is happening in the first place. ***

✦ Once students spot the argument, they can move on to identifying the type of argument as well. In the arguments above, there are arguments by example, arguments by sign, arguments by authority, arguments by analogy and others.

47. FALLACY FANTASY LAND

GOAL:

To give students a fun way to understand and apply various logical fallacies.

METHOD:

✦ Students assume the role of a fictional hero who must travel through a magic kingdom in order to find a treasure. Along the way, the hero is attacked by strange monsters that challenge her using fallacious arguments.

✦ The player must identify the fallacy in order to proceed.

For example, the player may draw a card on which a fierce troll is depicted saying: "You cannot proceed. None of the other heroes got past this point. They all stopped here, so you should stop here too!" If the student correctly identifies this fallacy as the **"Appeal to tradition"** then they get to proceed.

(Courtesy of Marcin Zeleski, president. I.D.E.A. For a complete version of this exercise email: mzaleski@lonet.gdynia.pl)

EXERCISES IN JUDGING

GOAL:
To give potential judges a detailed understanding debate.

METHOD:

✦ Present a debate recorded on videotape to potential judges.

✦ Instruct potential judges to flow the debate.

✦ Between speeches, the instructor can review the arguments, and check that judges are keeping accurate flows.

✦ The instructor can also teach by asking such questions as:

> **What is the most important argument at this point in the debate?**
>
> **Did you notice any mistakes in that last speech?**
>
> **What is the biggest challenge for the next speaker?**

✦ After the debate, instruct judges to work in small groups, go through the steps of reaching a decision:

> **Deciding on an interpretation**
>
> **Identifying important concessions**
>
> **Identifying important issues**
>
> **Resolving each issue**
>
> **Putting issues together to reach a decision**

✦ Judges should think about the positive and negative criticism that they would offer each team.

✦ The instructor can compare the results, stressing that there is not necessarily a correct decision, but that there are better and worse ways of arriving at a decision.

GOAL:

To provide an activity for a potential judge who is at a tournament, but not yet ready to judge.

METHOD:

✦ In addition to the official judge or judges at a debate, ask potential future judges to attend for training.

✦ Give them a ballot, and encourage them to flow the debate, reach a decision, and assign points, just as they would if they were actually judging.

✦ After the round, encourage the actual judges and the potential judges to discuss any differences they may have had. Emphasize that there is no correct decision, and even if the trainee judges disagree with the actual judges, it doesn't mean that one is right and the other wrong.

✦ The goal is to focus on the process of reaching a decision, and to increase the confidence and experience level of new judges.

**EXERCISES
IN JUDGING**

GOAL:

To initiate a discussion with new judges or with experienced judges on the difficulties of reaching a reasonable decision.

METHOD:

✦ For purposes of discussion, invent hypothetical situations that present judges with difficult choices. For example:

> **Affirmative's criterion is individualism, and the negative's is rule of law. Both sides have supported their criterion, but the debaters have not challenged each other's criteria. According to affirmative's criterion, affirmative wins, according to negative's criterion, negative wins. Which criterion would you accept?**
>
> **Affirmative uses an historical example to make their point. Based on your own knowledge, you realize that they have their facts wrong. Negative, unfortunately, does not realize this and fails to contest the example's accuracy. Do you accept affirmative's use of the example?**

✦ The point of this exercise is to encourage discussion and to demonstrate that some considerations are basic matters of fairness while other depend on the judge's own style.

NOTES:

Appendix 3
Sample Flows

FIRST AFFIRMATIVE

Definitions

"SOFT DRUGS" = cannabis, marijuana

"LEGALIZATION" = allowed or required by law

Criterion

Good of the community

Views on marijuana are shaped by prejudices and cultural beliefs, not facts

- There is a double standard in treating soft drugs worse than alcohol & cigarettes

I. Free Choice
-Choice is the basis of democratic society

- The state has a limited right to interfere

- not justified for marijuana because:
  1. Smoking marijuana doesn't hurt others' rights
  2. Marijuana isn't harmful enough

II. Pragmatic Benefits
A. Individual benefits

- quality controls

- price controls

- avoidance of "forbidden fruit" appeal

FIRST NEGATIVE

We accept the criterion

-No evidence proves cigarettes and alcohol are more harmful than soft drugs

- Even if they are as harmful as soft drugs, that doesn't justify adding more harms

The state has the right to limit choice

- Article 16 of Croatia's constitution:
  - health, public morality, and well-being justify limits

- Freedom requires responsibility

- State power to limit choice doesn't create risk - U.S.A. drug policy hasn't hurt democracy

- drugs aren't of high quality

- lower prices on harmful things is bad

- If theft was legal, then more people would steal

SECOND AFFIRMATIVE

-Free choice is the most basic principle of a democracy

-You should have the right to decide as long as you don't hurt others

-Quality controls work in Netherlands

-Price control means a fair price and no "middle man"

-Theft can't be compared to soft drugs; theft endangers people

SECOND NEGATIVE

-Drugs are harmful enough to stop people from having a right to choose

THIRD AFFIRMATIVE

-Negative promotes paternalism (treating citizens as children)

*Oxford Dictionary
-paternalism=
-controlling & denying responsibility and freedom of choice

They did not refute the pragmatic benefits

THIRD NEGATIVE

-Democracy doesn't mean anarchy

-Government still has a right to control in a democracy-people should not be ermitted to risk themselves

-Example: seatbelts

-Legalization isn't necessary for democracy (all democratic countries but Holland ban drugs)

-Laws set a standard for what is good and what is normal

148

B. Community benefits

- Taxes

- Reallocation of resources toward hard drugs, education

- Demystification, and destigmatization. We should be able to talk about soft drugs and we shouldn't treat users as criminals

---

Decrease in Black Market

Legalization will separate the markets for soft drugs and hard drugs

---

- The state shouldn't receive money for harming health

It is better for soft drugs to remain un-normal, and to remain banned

---

Legalization will mean more benefits for those who own the drug market

---

I. Harm to individuals
a. physiological harms: brain damage, memory, learning, heart, reproduction, motor, immunological system
b. psychological harms: Toxic psychosis, panic, schizophrenia, depersonalization

---

II. Harm to society
a. Soft drugs offer escapism
b. Society requires responsible citizens
c. Soft drugs are ego-ist, & benefit no one

- State money can be beneficially used & reallocated

- 1/3 of prisoners in W. Europe are in for drug crimes

- People who use shouldn't be regarded as bad-guys

- Marijuana has good uses: arthritis, glaucooma

- There would be a decrease in the black market

- Yes, soft drugs can cause harms when abused

- Other things are also harmful (cigarettes, alcohol, fatty foods)

- Can still be regulated even if legalized

- They haven't shown how extreme the psychological effects are

---

- Escapism is normal

- Free choice benefits society, it is not selfish

- We don't have a right to choose if "big father" chooses for us

---

- The state shouldn't get money from harms to its citizens Slavery was profitable, but not moral

---

- There's no such thing as soft drug "use," only "abuse" Drugs are only used to get high "Dr. Zuckerman says marijuana causes anxiety, panic, memory loss, more chemicals than cigarettes

- marijuana also causes heart rate increase, harms to reproductive problems & motor skills

---

- They admit that drug use makes people less rational

- Legalization means that users would increase - example of prohibition in U.S.A., and liberalization in Czech Republic (Newsweek)

- Irrational behavior makes people less responsible (example, U.S.A. in the 60's)

- "Use" means to employ for a purpose, so using marijuana to get high is still use, not necessarily abuse
- "Abuse" means excessive

- They don't say how much marijuana is necessary to produce these effects
- Same effects are caused by other things (drinking, parachuting)

- Prohibition also created black market and mafia and it was abolished

- Legalization just gives the right to choose, it doesn't force people to use marijuana So, there will not be an increase in use

- People use drugs because of psychological curiosity and rebellion Legalizing lessens both motives

Escapism is normal

- Marijuana is only used to get high, there is no such thing as using it for the right reasons

Just because there are other bad things isn't an excuse to add one more bad thing

---

- Affirmative assumes that users would be responsible, that they won't misuse or drive

- Legalizing opens Pandora's box

- They can't promote responsibility by making citizens irrational with soft drugs

1A: FIRST AFFIRMATIVE 6 minutes	1N: FIRST NEGATIVE 6 minutes	2A: SECOND AFFIRMATIVE 5 minutes
Agree with resolution	Disagree with resolution	Reaffirm position
Define the terms of the resolution	Agree with or offer alternative definitions	If necessary, reaffirm definitions/refute alternatives
Set goal or criterion	Accept goal or criterion or provide alternative	Reestablish goal or criterion
Establish prima facie case using an outline format I. First Argument II. Second Argument III. Third Argument (The number of arguments may vary)	Address each affirmative argument following the affirmative structure	Rebuild affirmative case using original structure. • Introduce new evidence • Recall critical aspects of previous evidence • Use examples, analogies, narratives • Extend existing arguments
	Introduce negative constructive case I. First Argument II. Second Argument (The number of arguments may vary)	Refute negative constructive arguments • Offer new evidence • Explain / expose flaws in negative's case • Use examples, analogies, narratives
Conclude with clear vision of affirmative position	Conclude by identifying main areas of clash	Conclude by identifying main areas of clash
Cross Examines 2N	Cross Examines 2A	Questioned by 1N

EACH TEAM HAS A TOTAL OF 8 MINUTES OF PREPARATION TIME.

2N: SECOND NEGATIVE
5 minutes

Clarify basic differences between sides

If arguing alternative definitions, further defend

If necessary, argue alternative goal or criterion.

Go through affirmative case point by point.

- Offer new evidence
- Explain / expose flaws in affirmative's case
- Use examples, analogies, narratives

Rebuild negative case using original structure

- Introduce new evidence
- Recall critical aspects of previous evidence
- Use examples, analogies, narratives
- Extend existing arguments

Questioned by 1A

3A: THIRD AFFIRMATIVE
5 minutes

Focus debate on decisive issues

Clarify any remaining controversy surrounding definitions

Show how the affirmative criterion or goal prevails

Go through affirmative and negative cases identifying and explaining key issues:

- Identify and weigh critical arguments for the judge
- Explain importance of critical arguments
- Clearly explain affirmative position on key arguments

Final Conclusion

Cross Examines 1N

3N: THIRD NEGATIVE
5 minutes

Focus debate on decisive issues

Clarify any remaining controversy surrounding definitions

Show how the negative criterion or goal prevails

Go through affirmative and negative cases identifying and explaining key issues:

- Identify and weigh critical arguments for the judge
- Explain and justify disagreement with affirmative on identity of key issues.
- Explain importance of critical arguments
- Clearly explain negative position on key arguments

Final Conclusion

EVERYONE SHAKES HANDS!

Cross Examines 1A

INFORMATION GAINED THROUGH CROSS-EXAMINATION SHOULD BE USED DURING SUBSEQUENT SPEECHES

Ad Hominem Argument

An attempt to discredit an argument by focusing on the character or qualifications of someone who supports it; an argument that appeals to personal prejudices or emotions rather than reason.

Affirmative Constructive

The first speech in a debate round, delivered by the affirmative team. In this speech the team makes its case in full, presenting all the reasons for accepting the resolution. Although the team may repeat points and expand on them in later sections of the debate, they may not introduce a new criterion, arguments, or definitions at a later time.

Affirmative Team

The team in a debate round that is arguing in favor of the resolution.

Analogy

A correspondence in a particular respect between two otherwise dissimilar things or events.

Argument

A claim supported by explanation and evidence.

Arguing Both Sides

The requirement in educational debate that a team argue both the affirmative and the negative side of a particular resolution during a debate tournament.

Ballot

The instrument used by debate judges to indicate which team has prevailed in a competition. Judges use the ballot to communicate the reasons behind their decision, identifying arguments that seemed especially strong or weak, addressing specific aspects of the debate, and commenting on style and performance.

Begging the Question

An assertion disguised as an argument, also known as a circular argument, or a tautology.

Brainstorming

A process for developing ideas or problem solving whereby members of a group spontaneously contribute ideas without self-editing or initial concern over the relevance of each contribution.

Burden of Proof

The responsibility of proving a disputed charge or allegation. In Karl Popper Debate, both sides have the burden of proof. In a criminal proceeding in the United States, by contrast, the state carries the burden of proof. Prosecutors must prove that that the accused is guilty. The accused must only demonstrate that the prosecution's case is not valid, but need not affirmatively demonstrate innocence.

Capital Punishment

The death penalty; execution by the state as punishment for a crime or a "capital offense."

Case

A complete set of arguments that includes an articulation of the terms of the resolution, statement of a criterion, and contention(s) in support of a position.

Civil Disobedience
The refusal to obey civil (as opposed to criminal) laws regarded as unjust, usually by employing methods of passive resistance.

Claim
In Toulmin's system of logic, the position the speaker wants to prove. The claim corresponds to the debater's position in favor or against the resolution. Compare the terms "warrant" and "grounds."

Clash
A direct response to a particular argument of the opponent's team.

Conclusion
In debate, the final comments of a case or speech. In Aristotelian logic, the third part of a syllogism, following the minor premise and the major premise.

Contention
A main argument that supports the case and which may in turn be supported by several minor arguments.

Corollary
A proposition that follows with little or no proof necessary from one already proven; a natural consequence, a result.

Criterion
(pl. Criteria). A standard by which something is judged, a primary value. In debate, a criterion is the standard by which a team can be said to have proven or disproven the resolution. For example, one criterion for judging the talent of a singer is by his or her vocal range.

Cross-Examination
The section of a debate in which speakers are questioned by opponents. See also First Affirmative Cross-Examination, Second Affirmative Cross-Examination, etc.

Debatable Proposition
A proposition over which reasonable people can disagree, not a statement of pure fact, faith, or opinion.

Deduction
The process of reasoning in which a conclusion follows necessarily from the stated premises; inference by reasoning from the general to the specific.

Democracy
A form of government in which political power is exercised either directly by citizens or by their representatives.

Diction
In speech, the degree of clarity and distinctness of pronunciation.

Dropping an Argument
Leaving an argument from the opposing team unanswered.

Educational Debate
A form of debate designed to increase student ability in critical thinking and presentation; characterized by formality of structure, restriction of conflict, and competitive judgment.

Elimination Rounds
The rounds in a tournament in which the winning teams advance and losing teams do not, e.g. quarter-finals, semi-finals.

Evidence
The support for an argument, often in the form of a quotation from an authority or other citation.

Fallacy
A fault in reasoning that makes an argument invalid.

First Affirmative Cross-Examination
The fourth part of a debate round, in which the third affirmative debater asks questions and the first negative debater responds. The negative debater may make concessions, but it is incumbent upon the affirmative team to capitalize on these concessions. Judges are not expected to see the significance of such concessions on their own.

First Affirmative Rebuttal
The fifth part of a debate round, in which the second affirmative speaker delivers her team's refutations of the first negative arguments and responds to the refutations made by the negative team. If the affirmative speaker does not refute a given point in the negative case, then that point stands; if the affirmative speaker does not respond to a particular negative objection, then that objection is conceded.

First Negative Cross-Examination
The second part of a debate round, in which the third negative debater asks questions and the first affirmative debater responds. The affirmative debater may make concessions, but it is incumbent upon the negative team to capitalize on these concessions. Judges are not expected to see the significance of such concessions on their own.

First Negative Rebuttal
The seventh part of debate round, in which the second negative speaker responds to the refutations made by the second affirmative and attacks the affirmative case. At this point in the debate, the negative speaker may start to draw the judge's attention to arguments that have been dropped. The negative speaker is not allowed to introduce completely new arguments at this point; previous arguments, however, may be revised, rephrased, or expanded.

Flow (vb. Flowing)
The progress of a debate, from point to point, through the sequences of arguments, and questions, and rebuttals. The verb form–to flow the debate–means to record the essential points of the debate, using columns for each speech, on paper as it proceeds. Both debaters and judges should flow a debate.

Flow Chart
A chart made by dividing a piece of paper into columns corresponding to the sections of a debate. In each column, the points made in a particular section are briefly noted. Horizontal lines can be used to visually connect contentions with refutations. The flow chart helps the debater keep track of arguments presented, and provides a summary of progress. See Appendix 3 for a sample flow chart.

Goal
A desired objective.

Grounds:
In Toulmin's system of logic, that which supports an argument. Compare the terms "warrant" and "claim."

Hasty generalization
A generalization based on too few atypical examples.

Induction
A process of reasoning in which a conclusion is reached by generalizing from particular examples or instances to broader conclusions.

Instructing the judge
To explicitly bring an argument to the judges' attention.

Issue
A question answered differently by the two sides and which matters in resolving the debate.

Judge
The person who decides which team has won a debate based on the analysis of the round. Judges' decisions should be based on an analysis of the round. A preliminary debate requires at least one judge, while elimination rounds require three or more judges.

Karl Popper
A noted philosopher who was born in Austria and spent most of his life teaching and writing in England. Author of *The Open Society and its Enemies* (1945), Popper said that he believed in the existence of absolute truth, but was suspicious of anyone who claimed to possess it.

Karl Popper Debate Format
A structured form of educational debate in which each round is divided into 10 distinct sections, each with its own rules, and each limited to a specific length of time. The Karl Popper Debate Format requires two teams with three members each.

Leading question
A question that is structured in such a way as to suggest an answer.

M-Chart
A three-column chart used as a more structured form of brainstorming. See "T-Chart."

NATO
North Atlantic Treaty Organization.

Negative Constructive
The third part of a debate round, in which the negative team offers a complete case against the resolution. Also used to begin refuting the affirmative arguments. If affirmative's definitions are not challenged at this point, they must stand. Similarly, if negative does not offer a competing criterion, it is assumed that the criterion articulated by affirmative will govern the round. The negative team must challenge affirmative contentions, otherwise it is assumed that they are acceptable.

Negative Team
The team in a debate round that is arguing against the resolution.

Non Sequitur
A statement that does not follow logically from the statement that precedes it.

Oral Critique
The criticisms and comments a judge gives at the end of a debate round.

Post Hoc, Ergo Propter Hoc
Latin words meaning, "after this, therefore because of this." A logical fallacy that holds that just because one event follows another, it was also caused by that first event.

Preliminary Rounds
Debate rounds that take place prior to elimination rounds.

Preparation Time
Time set aside to prepare arguments for debate, and time taken within a debate round itself to prepare rebuttal, cross-examination, or for other reasons. The preparation time in Karl Popper Debate Format is 8 minutes per team.

Prohibition
The period in the United States during which the sale and manufacture of alcohol was forbidden by law, 1920 to 1933.

Rebuttal
In debate, a speech in which a debater restates and extends previous arguments to respond to an opponent's arguments.

Rebut
To respond to a refutation by offering opposing arguments which support original arguments.

Refute
To deny the accuracy or truth of an opposing argument.

Resolution
The proposition with which debaters either agree or disagree.

Role-Playing
In debate preparation, an exercise during which members of the same team assume different roles—judge, the opposite team, audience—in order to anticipate the opposing team's reactions and arguments.

Second Affirmative Cross-Examination
The eighth part of a debate round, in which the first affirmative speaker questions the second negative speaker. See "First Affirmative Cross-Examination."

Second Affirmative Rebuttal
The ninth part of a debate round, in which the third affirmative speaker renews refutations that have not been addressed adequately and points out flaws in the second negative rebuttal. The debater rebuts refutations that have been kept alive by negative in its last speech. At this point, most good debaters will try to focus the judge's attention on the key issues of the round.

Second Negative Cross-Examination:
The sixth part of a debate round, in which the first negative speaker questions the second affirmative speaker.

Second Negative Rebuttal
The tenth and last part of a debate round, the second negative rebuttal is similar to the second affirmative rebuttal. Judges must be especially wary of speakers introducing new arguments at this point. Of course, a new argument would have been illegal in the first rebuttal made earlier; an illegal argument made at that point, however, could have been flagged by the affirmative team in its rebuttal. Now, the affirmative ream has no chance to respond, so a new argument is especially unfair. The judge must ignore any new arguments that are introduced.

Slippery slope
A logical fallacy that presumes that a chain of events will result because of one single action.

Sophistry
A seemingly plausible but ultimately misleading or logically flawed argument.

Speaker Points
The total number of points a debater receives from a judge in a debate round. In the Karl Popper Debate Format there is a maximum of 30 points.

Stonewall
A refusal to respond to questions.

Strategy
A plan of action designed to achieve an overall outcome.

Syllogism
Deductive reasoning from the general to the specific, formally consisting of a minor premise, a major premise, and a conclusion.

Tactics
The means employed toward achieving an end designated by strategy.

T-Chart
A chart shaped like the letter "T." Used in educational debate to structure brainstorming. Debaters draw a large letter "T" in their notebooks. On the left side of the vertical, they list positive ideas; on the right side of the vertical, negative ideas. The aim is to create complementary pairs.

Time Signals
Hand gestures, or written or oral statements indicating how much time remains in a speech.

Toulmin, Stephen
Twentieth century British philosopher who developed an approach to logic similar to Aristotle's, but distinctly different in significant ways, emphasizing informed public reasoning.

Validity
The soundness of the connection between evidence and claim.

Value Debate
Debate that involves the discussion and comparison of ideals toward which people strive.

Venn Diagram
A pictorial diagram using circles and other shapes to represent an operation in set theory. Most commonly seen as two circles overlapping to create a common area.

Voting Issues
Central conflicts in a debate that, once decided, will determine which team wins the competition.

Warrant
In Toulmin's system of logic, an arguable position. The warrant corresponds to the premise of a classic syllogism. The warrant can be understood as an underlying principle, as the idea that connects the claim with its support, the grounds of the argument. Toulmin emphasizes that the warrant itself must be established and cannot be taken as given.

Index.